A PUZZLED
MIND

Recovering Memories From Childhood Trauma

A practical survivor's guide for empaths that
examines how to deal with resurfacing memories
as a part of the spiritual awakening process

AnnCeline Dagger

BALBOA.PRESS

A DIVISION OF HAY HOUSE

Balboa Press books may be ordered through booksellers or by contacting:

Balboa Press
A Division of Hay House
1663 Liberty Drive
Bloomington, IN 47403
www.balboapress.com
844-682-1282

Because of the dynamic nature of the Internet, any web addresses or links contained in this book may have changed since publication and may no longer be valid. The views expressed in this work are solely those of the author and do not necessarily reflect the views of the publisher, and the publisher hereby disclaims any responsibility for them.

The author of this book does not dispense medical advice or prescribe the use of any technique as a form of treatment for physical, emotional, or medical problems without the advice of a physician, either directly or indirectly. The intent of the author is only to offer information of a general nature to help you in your quest for emotional and spiritual well-being. In the event you use any of the information in this book for yourself, which is your constitutional right, the author and the publisher assume no responsibility for your actions.

Any people depicted in stock imagery provided by Getty Images are models, and such images are being used for illustrative purposes only.
Certain stock imagery © Getty Images.

Print information available on the last page.

ISBN: 978-1-9822-6586-1 (sc)
ISBN: 978-1-9822-6587-8 (e)

Balboa Press rev. date: 03/25/2021

CONTENTS

ACKNOWLEDGMENTS

I wrote this book after waking up to realizations regarding past traumas that I had been left to figure out alone. Adult survivors remembering trauma after experiencing trigger events may not have the luxury of finding people who will confirm what happened. On many occasions, the victims and abusers are the only ones who know. I wrote this book for survivors, to shed some light on your questions and confirm the suspicions you've always had about certain events.

A big thank you goes to my closest friends and family who have stuck with me so far, didn't give up on me, and supported me on this journey. Another big thank you goes to my therapists for finally explaining what had been going on in my life. And finally, thank you to all the intuitive healers who tried to help me remember my past.

As an adult, I finally found the support I needed as a child. I feel I owe most of my healing to my angels who have guided me since my early childhood. I therefore dedicate this survivor's guide to you, my guardian angels. Without you, I would truly have been all alone.

Thank you,

AnnCeline

MISSION STATEMENTS

- I don't agree with missions or labeling anything, but I do feel personally responsible for sharing my experiences with people who need to hear them before I depart from this world.
- Taking charge of our own health on all levels—mental, physical, emotional, and spiritual—allows us to become the best versions of ourselves as we take back our God-given power.
- The power to heal and integrate is already within us.
- Trust that anything is possible.
- Trust in divine timing and effortless unfoldment.
- We realize our own superpowers once we make the decision to connect to ourselves and allow for the unfoldment of our divine plan.
- Your life will transform when you are ready.
- You have the power to change your own story.
- I'm here to help you realize the things you were too afraid to consider, to allow yourself to open your mind and heart to the possibilities.
- My passion is to assist sensitive people along their path of self-realization.
- Alone we are vulnerable, but together we can help each other to grow and thrive.
- I'm here to help lead others to their own freedom from programming and manipulation.

I decided to write this book after I was left scrambling for answers to explain the things I was experiencing. I found answers in many places, but true guidance regarding how to heal was something I learned only by connecting with my soul and with my angels.

PEARLS OF WISDOM: A DREAM

I am surrounded by a deep blue ocean, floating freely. Am I drowning? An oxygen mask appears out of nowhere, and I put it over my face. Now I can breathe again.

Where am I? I turn myself around under the water as sunlight breaks through the surface of the sea and brightens the area below me. I begin to descend toward the ocean floor. Fear of not having enough air crosses my mind for a second, but I feel it's safe and I can trust.

The descent is difficult. I feel myself struggling to swim lower, but ocean currents keep pushing me back toward the surface. Why am I trying to go lower? I feel there's a treasure, maybe a chest filled with gold. Something incredibly special is hiding at the bottom of the ocean, waiting for me to discover it.

I am seeing dolphins and coral on my way down. As I go lower, the light is dimming, but I feel drawn to keep going. I'm not afraid, because the water is me.

There are large shells buried in the rocks. I have a small pick with me and begin to use it to open one shell, believing that there may be beautiful pearls inside. I feel excited and ecstatic.

The shell isn't easy to open, and my pick breaks. With some hard work, I'm able to open the shell. Light is coming through the water and shining directly at the treasure I find inside the shell. There are three pearls: a black one, a white one, and a pinkish gold one.

INTRODUCTION

Thank you for choosing to read this book. It's the first book I've ever written. It has been a passion of mine and was initially born from pain and confusion.

As I was writing, I was growing from the third-dimensional lower levels into the higher fourth-, fifth-, and sixth-dimensional levels of consciousness. In layman's terms, I was growing my awareness during the writing process. You'll notice as you read that some sections may seem like they're written by a different person. I intentionally left the sections that way.

Why? I wanted you to see the growth I've undergone and the levels of understanding I was acquiring during the time I wrote the manuscript. I wanted you to see for yourself just what is possible if you follow the steps I've taken through this process of awakening and remembering trauma. I not only grew from a newly aware victim into a survivor but also began to thrive, and from that point I grew into an evolved and unified high-consciousness being. I woke up.

It's about much more than just remembering your trauma and the past. In my case, it was also about remembering who I really was at my core, my true authentic self, my higher or greater self. I was becoming wide open to universal consciousness and the trueness of my being. There are no words to describe what I am or who I am. I simply am. I am one with God.

CHAPTER 1

The Awakening Journey

WHEN WE EXPERIENCE EMOTIONAL TRIGGERS or other circumstances that simulate traumatic events from our childhoods, we will sometimes experience what I call an *awakening journey*. Childhood traumas that were severe enough to be rejected by the mind will resurface after getting triggered into a spiritual awakening. It begins with feelings of loss or hopelessness—a sense that the other shoe will drop or that some disaster is about to happen—followed by a need to figure out who you are. Confusion triggers your mind to check into your own memories. You may experience multiple incidents of déjà vu per day; derealization and depersonalization; and a sense of losing yourself. This leads to feeling as if you need to go find yourself.

Scientists in Sweden have discovered a mechanism inside the brain that simply rejects certain experiences if they can't be categorized or don't fit into your reality. When you begin to recall repressed memories, you may notice a sudden activation of your survival instincts, intense fear, or a fear of death, which can be a memory. Or your intuition may heighten, and you may even experience premonitions. The memories may re-emerge suddenly but immediately be rejected by your mind because of their dreamlike appearance.

You've most likely been doing this for decades, but now your heart may have broken open, and the barriers or blocks you'd built up are diminishing. You'll be much more aware of it happening now that you're paying attention. This will make you feel like you're losing your mind, but you're not. You're going to regain the missing links and memories of your childhood. Déjà vu is your multidimensional self experiencing the present moment as a memory of the past or the future.

I'm going to explain to you the process of fragmented-memory recalling and how I've experienced this part of the awakening journey. I wanted to write my life story, but I felt it was important to first create this survivor's guide, as I noticed that a large percentage of the earth's population was experiencing the awakening process. This is a vital part of your survival, and it's important that you don't feel as if you're the only one who's having to experience this phenomenon. If you're a very intuitive person, this process will be especially confusing, because it will combine with your abilities to perceive life from a different perspective.

Many intuitive healers and psychics have experienced severe abuse as children. This is not the cause of your abilities, but it complicated things and sensitized you because you needed to be on extra-high alert. Your greatest sufferings and hardships have the potential to become your greatest sources of strength and power.

At some point on your awakening and healing journey, you will come to the realization that you have chosen to take this life on as yours, and you'll begin to understand that "everything is here to help you," as Matt Kahn said. It can be difficult to see this concept from a place of victimhood, pain, and suffering, but as you grow, I know you'll find this truth along your own journey. There really are light, joy, happiness, and peace of mind at the end of the tunnel. In fact, that's your natural state of being, which you'll regain when you relearn to trust yourself.

A healer is born out of the depths of a muddy pond. Her ability to heal herself will determine her abilities to help heal the world.

Recovering fragmented and dreamlike memories was extremely confusing to me. These were not only memories of my childhood trauma resurfacing. Memories of psychics I came in contact with as a child and young adult resurfaced at the same time, including some memories of in-between lives before I was born, of meeting and talking to angels as a young child, and even some of my own future. Imagine the confusion of trying to figure everything out.

Three years into this awakening process, I've come to many realizations, and now I feel it's time to share this for all of you, my fellow empaths and survivors of childhood trauma. Your awakening begins the day you start to question your reality.

CHAPTER 1

The Awakening Journey

WHEN WE EXPERIENCE EMOTIONAL TRIGGERS or other circumstances that simulate traumatic events from our childhoods, we will sometimes experience what I call an *awakening journey*. Childhood traumas that were severe enough to be rejected by the mind will resurface after getting triggered into a spiritual awakening. It begins with feelings of loss or hopelessness—a sense that the other shoe will drop or that some disaster is about to happen—followed by a need to figure out who you are. Confusion triggers your mind to check into your own memories. You may experience multiple incidents of déjà vu per day; derealization and depersonalization; and a sense of losing yourself. This leads to feeling as if you need to go find yourself.

Scientists in Sweden have discovered a mechanism inside the brain that simply rejects certain experiences if they can't be categorized or don't fit into your reality. When you begin to recall repressed memories, you may notice a sudden activation of your survival instincts, intense fear, or a fear of death, which can be a memory. Or your intuition may heighten, and you may even experience premonitions. The memories may re-emerge suddenly but immediately be rejected by your mind because of their dreamlike appearance.

You've most likely been doing this for decades, but now your heart may have broken open, and the barriers or blocks you'd built up are diminishing. You'll be much more aware of it happening now that you're paying attention. This will make you feel like you're losing your mind, but you're not. You're going to regain the missing links and memories of your childhood. Déjà vu is your multidimensional self experiencing the present moment as a memory of the past or the future.

I'm going to explain to you the process of fragmented-memory recalling and how I've experienced this part of the awakening journey. I wanted to write my life story, but I felt it was important to first create this survivor's guide, as I noticed that a large percentage of the earth's population was experiencing the awakening process. This is a vital part of your survival, and it's important that you don't feel as if you're the only one who's having to experience this phenomenon. If you're a very intuitive person, this process will be especially confusing, because it will combine with your abilities to perceive life from a different perspective.

Many intuitive healers and psychics have experienced severe abuse as children. This is not the cause of your abilities, but it complicated things and sensitized you because you needed to be on extra-high alert. Your greatest sufferings and hardships have the potential to become your greatest sources of strength and power.

At some point on your awakening and healing journey, you will come to the realization that you have chosen to take this life on as yours, and you'll begin to understand that "everything is here to help you," as Matt Kahn said. It can be difficult to see this concept from a place of victimhood, pain, and suffering, but as you grow, I know you'll find this truth along your own journey. There really are light, joy, happiness, and peace of mind at the end of the tunnel. In fact, that's your natural state of being, which you'll regain when you relearn to trust yourself.

A healer is born out of the depths of a muddy pond. Her ability to heal herself will determine her abilities to help heal the world.

Recovering fragmented and dreamlike memories was extremely confusing to me. These were not only memories of my childhood trauma resurfacing. Memories of psychics I came in contact with as a child and young adult resurfaced at the same time, including some memories of in-between lives before I was born, of meeting and talking to angels as a young child, and even some of my own future. Imagine the confusion of trying to figure everything out.

Three years into this awakening process, I've come to many realizations, and now I feel it's time to share this for all of you, my fellow empaths and survivors of childhood trauma. Your awakening begins the day you start to question your reality.

CHAPTER 2
Extrasensory Abilities

ARE WE BORN WITH EXTRASENSORY abilities, or does the abuse we suffered bring them on? Many empaths I've encountered have wondered about this. I feel this question relates to which came first: the chicken or the egg? In my opinion, you are who you are. Your abilities are a part of you and always have been, through all times and existences.

We are in fact multidimensional beings. I feel most people have psychic abilities, but they're dormant and inactivated. When we experience severe abuse or a very confusing situation, like mental manipulation and emotional neglect, our curious spirits will want to understand this. So we go deep to look for the reason why, even as children.

Due to the complexity of trauma and the fear-based hormone responses in our bodies, we often reject our experiences because they can't be categorized by the young mind, nor can we recall the details adequately. This puts us to sleep, so to speak. It causes dissociation, but it also makes us hypervigilant. We're looking for signs and clues to warn us about potential danger or to stay a step ahead of our abusers.

Many of us who have experienced sexual abuse and rape as young children get thrown into an early awakening, where our spirit—in order to protect us—tries to make us wake up and remember our true nature so we can become aware. When activated, our dormant superpower travels through our bodies and unblocks us. It opens us up to greater awareness and eventually leads to full self-realization. It used to be thought of as something that only happened to yogis after thousands of hours of meditation, but these are changing times, and that paradigm has shifted.

Sexual abuse may in fact trigger this rise in energy, which lies coiled up and sleeping at the base of our spine. Once awakened, it will begin to do what it does. A burning sensation rises inside the lower energy centers and travels through the body along the spine until it reaches the top of the head and pours out. This stimulates very vivid imagination through hormonal activation and release inside the brain and pineal gland. You'll be seeing, hearing, and knowing things a young child couldn't possibly know. These awakenings will take their course and rewire the body to house a higher-consciousness being.

Many people I've talked to have experienced walk-ins at some point in their lives and can't recall anything before that fateful day. A walk-in usually happens when a person is in an unconscious state or in a state of utter panic, with no will to live. That's when higher-consciousness beings can enter.

This doesn't happen automatically; permission needs to be granted. A contract is formed in terms of, "I help you, and you help me." All parties must agree to be one life and experience. That was the approximate process I can recall being told about during my out-of-body experience when I was about 5 years old.

After talking to an organization overseas about my experience, which initially left me with plenty of self-doubt about the reality of it, I confirmed my suspicion that this is in fact commonly reported. Other survivors have confided in me the details of their out-of-body experiences during rapes, and all are remarkably similar. My own experiences have made me take an in-depth look at myself, my life, my situations, the psychology behind people, and what I've seen and felt within my own body. This includes how hidden trauma represents itself later in life and what the effects are of such experiences of complex trauma.

During my out-of-body experience, I didn't want to come back to this life, as I saw my body as damaged and unfitting. Yet I found that a part of my purpose and my gift to others is to share what I know. I wanted to do this for you because I saw goodness in human hearts and felt that this was worth saving, despite all the evil of the human mind and its systems. I see the truth behind the facade, the realness in your heart, the feelings and emotions, and the complexity of human life. I have compassion for you.

It's not an easy existence here as a human being. It certainly is complicated. My purpose is to shed light on the things most people are afraid to look at or even consider. By no means am I saying that I'm always accurate or have it all perfectly figured out. Honestly, nobody ever has. Every day, I receive new information and get new insights into the world, consciousness, and how the universe functions, and I realize that yesterday's truth may not be the same tomorrow.

All we see is a slice of the cake, and all truths are just partial truths. One person's truth is different from another's. When you accept that life is always changing and nothing ever stays the same—that even what we believe is a truth or a totality is in reality only a little drop out of the ocean—only then can you allow yourself to be open enough to see the truth in what I'm writing about in this book.

My views and opinions are only one slice of the cake, but they are just as valid as your slice. My writing today is today's truth that I have discovered. However, my truth may change tomorrow. I'm allowing for the continuous growth of my consciousness into higher realms.

When we ascend, our world changes with us. There's no separation between outer world and inner world anymore. Inner space is all there is, so I've taken down the mirrors I'd created and became a free spirit, completely unbound by conditioning, beliefs, rules, and regulations. I govern myself, and I'm always open to the new inspirations of my heart.

CHAPTER 3

Dirty Laundry

THE TOPIC OF CHILD RAPE is a really difficult one to address. Everyone still seems afraid to talk about it. This isn't a surprise, because we're always told that we shouldn't air our dirty laundry in public. We should keep quiet and not share personal experiences with others out of fear of what they might think or talk about behind our backs. We have been told that our memories are incorrect because they would out the family.

We got gaslighted as children. Gaslighting is dangerous behavior that contradicts people's trust in their own experiences and memories by denying their truth and using their words against them—shaming and guilt-tripping the victim. There's also the factor of cognitive dissonance: the belief in a reality that contradicts the truth of what's really happening. The mind often goes into denial. Unable to comprehend the truth, it dismisses that information entirely. This makes it difficult to talk about sensitive subjects. An open and curious mind is of the essence here.

As a child exposed to gaslighting, you'll experience self-esteem issues and feelings of worthlessness well into adulthood. You were manipulated into thinking that the issues were *your* dirty laundry, not the abuser's. That's why you were not supposed talk about it.

Well, let me tell you: being sexually, emotionally, mentally, or physically abused was never your fault. And if it wasn't your fault, it isn't your dirty laundry. You've essentially been covering up someone else's dirty laundry because you got brainwashed. Gaslighting creates huge contradictions, and this distorts one's sense of reality and awareness.

Pedophilia

Pedophilia is a serious condition that affects many people. It isn't something that people outgrow; in fact, it becomes worse with age if not properly treated. Pedophilia and resulting attacks on children are seriously punished in many countries. However, unfortunately, many pedophiles are never caught, because the cases are often difficult to prove. Some are covered up by pedophiles and criminals in positions of authority and influence. This guarantees that abusers are never brought to justice, since they can directly influence police reporting, medical histories, and legal procedures.

I'm referring here to organized child sex-trafficking rings or pedophile organizations. These aren't necessarily global and can operate in small towns, families, and clubs. Many people think of child molesters and traffickers as typical smeary, unkempt guys in leather jackets or with gang colors, but that's just an image they want you to believe so they can keep doing their evil work.

Unbeknownst by you, it's the friendly man who helped your kid get into the fire truck at the fair, or your favourite uncle who's well educated, runs his own business, and freely gives to his family to support them. Whatever you believe it is, most likely the truth is the complete opposite. Abusers are incredible at coercing, convincing, and pretending, and most of the time, you'd never guess that they lied straight to your face.

It's been reported that abusers literally had sex with a child right in front of the parents and they didn't notice. There are multiple accounts and videos available online from police departments that speak about this process of using distraction, just like a magician would do. Years later, your child will tell you about it, and you won't believe it because you were there and didn't see anything suspicious.

Yes, you didn't see it, because the abuser tricked you, and your child believed for years that you were okay with what this person did. Usually, this causes huge rifts in families. Victims may end up never speaking to their parents or family members because they feel a lack of transparency and worry about getting manipulated and abused again. They also worry about their own children coming in contact with a family dynamic that's unhealthy, manipulative, and abusive.

As a victim, you're going to have to decide for yourself what you feel comfortable with. However, being in or staying in contact with an abusive environment isn't going to help you on your healing journey. Even if the abusers didn't understand the effects of their actions or say that they don't remember what happened, the cycle of abuse can only be escaped one way, so choose wisely, even if it's hard.

Pedophiles are very aware of how the minds of young victims reject certain memories. They know exactly how it works, so if you're the victim, you have little chance of getting yourself out of this trap. Experts in the field agree that if you were sexually abused and groomed into compliance from a young age, you'll possibly never clue into it. If you do, your abuser will deny the truth, causing you to shut down.

If this abuse happens through a close caregiver you love, like a father or mother, there's a very high likelihood you'll completely repress all memories connected to the abuse perpetrated by this loved one. If you were abused by a cousin at age 11 but were also sexually groomed by your father, you may be able to recall the abuse by the cousin but completely repress the abusive memories of your father.

This is very typical behavior because your emotional connection to your father is greater than to your cousin. Your parents are your source of safety and security. To believe otherwise would cause an existential crisis that's incompatible with life as an adult and definitely as a child.

You may try to distract from the real problem by focusing on a lesser problem. It's easier for your mind to focus on the abuse by the cousin than to pay attention to the abuse by your parent. The mind will always go for what's easier to process first. You'll also realize that when you later recover memories from your childhood, the lighter and easier-to-digest problems will often reappear first, and then the rest of the story follows.

For example, if you're also open spiritually, it may be easier to recall the memories of angels or certain situations that seemingly made no sense than it is to recall the actual abuse, which represents severe trauma. If you tell friends about your memories, they might wonder why there seem to be more and more outrageous memories coming up and begin to doubt you, but I learned from my psychologists that this is actually a normal process.

Accepting the fact that this close person is dangerous to you will destroy your sense of safety, security, and reality. Your mind is unable to accept that without experiencing severe shock. Instead, your mind decides to repress those memories completely and live in denial, seeing this as the only way to avoid an existential crisis.

Here's an example of how I remember the experience of being in an abusive situation that took my memory. My abuser came in my room saying that he needed me. My initial response was silence, a sense that I couldn't move, shallow breathing, a rapid heart rate, and a feeling of ants running all over my body—mainly on my back, arms, and head. I was close to fainting. I felt dizzy, and I couldn't think or verbally respond. I was about 18 or 19, so this was still happening after many years of exposure to an abuser in my environment.

He asked me questions I couldn't answer, and I simply nodded in agreement, without defending myself or screaming. I'd been groomed, and my body knew how to respond to make it bearable. I felt unable to run, even if the thought had crossed my mind—running to the door, unlocking it, then screaming while running down the stairway. However, the bubble immediately popped when I realized that by the time I'd fiddled with the lock, he'd have caught up to me. There was no escaping. I'd tried that years earlier.

After he was done, he left and came back with money so I could go buy myself something nice. I got changed and stuck the money in my purse, thinking that if I never found a job, at least I could sell my body for money. He gave me four hundred dollars. It had also just been my birthday, so there was an excuse.

Minutes later, I found myself forgetting what had happened. I paused as I got dressed and looked at myself in the mirror. I saw a thin and pale young girl wearing baggy clothes. I could barely look at my eyes. I felt like scum. I felt unworthy of my own love. I hated myself. I found a million reasons why the girl in the mirror was the most disgusting creature on earth.

I went to the bathroom and puked out the apple I'd just eaten. That day, I wouldn't eat. I drank water and left, still unable to look in the mirror while going down in the elevator. I couldn't remember what had happened and looked at myself with concern. Was I losing it? I shrugged my shoulders, as I couldn't recall what had occurred and why I suddenly felt so unwell. I was looking forward to going out, meeting a friend, and having a couple of drinks at the local bar. I was looking forward to dancing, letting the fun and socializing take my darkness away, just for a few hours.

Dissociation is a key factor in why we can't recall trauma, but grooming from infancy is the real culprit in terms of why we don't clue in to what's really going on. Grooming is a form of manipulation—a method to train children into behaving a certain way. We often groom our children to be *nice*. To be nice means to comply with whatever is suggested by a person in authority or someone who needs you or needs help from you.

When you're groomed from such a young age, you'll never know that you're being manipulated into behaving in a certain way, and you'll likely never hear anyone explain what's being done to you. You're missing the words for it, since it's not a part of your vocabulary, and nobody ever asks you how you feel or helps you to articulate your feelings and the situations you've experienced. As an adult, this will often leave you incapable of speaking about your true feelings and what you need from a relationship or from life in general. We often end up serving our partners and help them achieve their best lives while we simply accompany them on the ride.

You may feel like you are cursed, but in fact, you were coerced. Sometimes it feels as if your life isn't your own or someone put a spell on you that keeps you from understanding yourself or accessing your own strength and power. You won't clue in that you got groomed, sexually abused, and manipulated until someone explains it, or you read a book about it, or you hear about such things in school. This may trigger your memory, and you may start to put two and two together.

Usually, you're a teenager by this point, but the minute you understand the crazy circumstances you're in, you'll truly be in danger. Abusers will do anything in their power to stop you from remembering or knowing what's going on. Some of us won't survive this.

I met a new friend at school, and we connected right away. I was about 15 years old, and we became close friends. At some point, she began to confide in me about sexual abuse she'd suffered from one of her uncles. She told me that she'd pushed away the memories and every time they resurfaced, she was pushing them away again, until one day something happened. When she was about 12, someone passed or there was a divorce, I can't remember exactly, but it triggered her abuse memories so that she was fully aware of them. She told her mom, who didn't want to believe her at first, but the authorities were contacted and it was investigated. Eventually, her mother began to believe her story.

My new friend turned to me and asked if anything like that had ever happened to me, since I seemed so much like her before she was aware of what had happened. I shook my head and told her that I didn't think so. At home that evening, I told my parents at the dinner table about our conversation, and they both looked worried. They told me I shouldn't hang around with that particular friend.

When I asked why, they replied that people like that weren't good for me. Abusers will try to manipulate you into not connecting with people who could potentially trigger your memory or make you realize what happened to you.

Complex trauma involves much more than just a one-time sexual act. It includes repeated emotional and mental trauma. Peeling back the layers of your problems today can lead you down the path of recovering the lost puzzle pieces of your memory. When a victim remembers the abuse decades later, looking for proof but finding no evidence, what will happen?

From my own experience, I can tell you that recovering memories is a difficult procedure that comes with plenty of self-doubt, because the process happens in steps or waves. It's difficult to grasp that memories return like puzzle pieces. You find them piece by piece across the floor and begin to ask yourself, and maybe your friends will ask you as well, why there are seemingly more and more memories and details emerging. Many friends will stop believing you because you keep coming up with more and more pieces of an incomplete and grotesque story, one that nobody really wants to hear.

This lack of empathy from others is extremely disturbing to an already sensitive being, and you may begin to feel like you're the bad person all over again, reconfirming your old feelings from childhood and reaffirming old realities. This often makes it difficult to dig up more of that dirt that's not really yours but has affected you and undermined you all your life.

Because of these different pieces of the puzzle, for some time your mind and your past will appear fragmented to you. Your mind only gives bits and pieces back at a time, which heavily influences your trust in yourself. Having friends and family doubt you won't make that any easier. When you look for proof and encounter resistance, denial, and lack of evidence, trust in yourself is difficult to establish. Self-doubt can strip the process of a puzzled mind's memory recall system, and the mind may just shut down the whole process.

I was only 15 years old when I read a book about a girl who became pregnant by her father, which I received at school. We were handed this book because they'd noticed that some children had missed out on sex education when they changed schools. I changed schools in 1995, and the new school had taught sex education the year before, but my old school didn't have it at that point.

Reading this book triggered my memories and made me understand the situation I was in. Yet when I brought it up and tried to tell people, I got smothered into compliance by my abusers. I was being denied my truth in order to cover up their crimes. They went as far as using alternative and hypnotic methods to try to suppress the emotions and physical pain from the experiences, naturally without telling the therapists about the true cause.

Twenty years later, my mind got triggered again, and the process restarted. However, this time I was thousands of kilometres away from my abusers, and I was an adult, capable of making sense of my memories—or at least today I can. At the beginning, I thought I must be losing my mind. Today, after years of putting the pieces of my mind back together, bit by bit like a puzzle, I fully understand and trust myself.

Some perverted minds are inventing new names for pedophilia, such as "minor attracted person." Pedophilia is *not* a sexual orientation, like being gay or bisexual. It's a severe crime and a mental illness that needs proper treatment.

Some people believe that this illness originated from people being subjected to sexual abuse as children, but they're wrong about that. According to statistics, most if not all abuse victims would *never* repeat their abuse by subjecting another person to it. However, their social behaviours may be affected due to unresolved resentment, anger, and unconscious re-enactments in relationships. This needs to be examined so you can become unified within and detach from what is not your true self and not your own authentic behaviour.

Abuse is often more about power than anything else. It may be accompanied by other agendas, such as money or sexual gratification, but it's usually about power—either over the partner or over a child—to compensate for the lack of power within the self. Personally, after talking to many survivors about this, I found that women and girls tend to become timid, shy, and insecure and occasionally lash out because of their suppressed anger. They may self-harm or engage in self-harming behaviour without realizing it, such as unsafe sexual contact or distracted driving.

Men can exhibit similar behaviour, but the ones I encountered were behaving in the opposite way to how women respond to hidden sexual trauma. Men often have a chip on their shoulder, are easily aggravated, and respond aggressively, often becoming narcissistic abusers. They may suffer from a Peter Pan complex—a child in an adult's body. They often have multiple sexual relationships with women to subconsciously prove that they aren't gay, or engage in adrenaline-fuelled activities like fast motorcycles and extreme sports. They often exhibit alpha male behaviour and lack empathy for others, although they appear to be sensitive and emotional men. This is just a loose description of patterns I've observed, which may not be complete or apply to everyone.

You've been programmed by dysfunction and thus need to work on removing that programming from your body and mind so you can live a joyous, beautiful, and manipulation-free life. Coercion takes time to heal. You have to recognize the programming, remember why it's there, and understand how it's affecting you in order to dissolve it.

The common belief that a stranger is usually the abuser of a child is incorrect. In most cases, abusers know their victims very well. European statistics indicate that the majority of child sexual abuse is conducted by people with close access to the child, such as a father, uncle, or brother. Even if they've never actually acted on their desires, these people are a walking time bomb. Appropriate psychological therapy and treatment is absolutely critical. It's irresponsible of us as a society not to take proper care of our sick. If we want a proper functioning society and healthy adults, it's imperative to have adequate psychological services that are readily available.

In my own opinion, I find that our nutrition influences our mental health. Eating a diet high in protein and fat from meat and animal products may be negatively influencing people's personalities. Once I became vegetarian, my mind calmed, and my anxiety greatly decreased. Eating meat is predatory and often leads to more predatory behaviour in a person, which may start with minor symptoms but could advance into something very unfavourable.

Sexual abuse has been prevalent since the dawn of mankind, and so has the practice of eating the flesh of other sentient beings. Can you see the connection behind it all? Just give this some thought. I know most people don't ever think that deeply about our current world problems, but it's important if we want to make solid changes for a better future.

To make changes that last and are beneficial, we need three key ingredients. These are higher awareness, deeper understanding, and transformation through the intention to change and grow our being.

Nuclear Blast

This is what happens to your mind when you're a child who is experiencing trauma. Children rely on parents to take care of them. Parents are their support and closest connection to a human being, but then something happens that the young mind can't categorize. It's something that's impossible to make sense of at that age. The adult responsible for you obviously won't explain, since it's far too much for a child to handle an adult issue.

Fear is a tool of coercion and manipulation. In a state of fear, your memory will freeze and then get shattered as if a bomb was dropped on the icy surface of shock and terror. This adds to the fragmentation and dreamlike appearance of your memories. Your mind becomes conflicted and confused. You're too young to make sense of it and to deal with all the fear and pain. This will trigger a panic attack.

I can remember the moment when my mind split into pieces. I was lying on my bed, unable to move my body, in shock. It felt like everything had become rigid within my body, mind, and heart—like I was trapped inside a piece of glass. There were many voices in my head, all talking at once about what was going on, but I couldn't understand them. I couldn't move or think one more step. It was so rigid. I couldn't breathe. And then it happened.

Boom!

Like a nuclear explosion that splits the atom, my mind was hit by a blast of realizations and split into pieces. The glass shattered as the nuclear bomb, representing the realization of my trauma, dropped on my mind's mirror image and split my memories into a thousand fragments. My mind became bilobed. Just as our brains have two sides, I now had two sides to my personality, meaning that my cognitive mind no longer communicated with my non-cognitive mind. This was the birth of AnnCeline.

The splitting of the self creates a life in separation, meaning that you may sometimes feel like you're switching personalities. You're not crazy. You experienced a complex trauma and have rejected parts of yourself and your experiences to protect you from the harshness of your reality. Rejecting parts of our experience seems to create a separation of personalities.

I feel this is a normal response to abnormal circumstances and a healthy way to protect yourself as a child. Simply put, it's a natural survival skill, which child abusers are highly aware of and are using in their favour. As an adult, you're going to unlearn that and change your trauma through working on your inner self and reintegrating the rejected parts to become whole again.

Crazy is a word people use to describe something they have an inability to comprehend. Lack of understanding leads to confusion, and hence the word *crazy* is used to describe that. There's a communication failure between the left brain and the right brain, or the conscious self and the unconscious self. This is simply a survival skill. Without this, you'd have to be fully aware of your trauma and live with that, which is not compatible with life. Splitting up the self is the only other option—at least until you're older and able to work through your traumas.

In healing work, we embrace the fragmented parts of our self, the parts we've rejected and pushed away, so we can integrate them all back into our being and feel whole again, a process that heals dissociation. We embrace all parts of ourselves, including our trauma and our positive experiences, in the same way—with love, empathy, and true compassion for ourselves and what we've been through.

Empathy can be a difficult skill to develop, particularly after not experiencing empathy toward ourselves and repeatedly being told that we must be pretending. Our feelings were repeatedly dismissed and not acknowledged by the ones we loved or who should have cared for us. It hardens us temporarily as we encapsulate ourselves for protection, until we allow ourselves to thaw and wake up.

Yet with the awakening, the inescapable memories and the truth about the past also return. Not everyone will go there, and not everyone will heal the same way. This is exactly where the world needs to learn more about empathy and compassion toward others so we can all heal from our collective traumas as much as our individual ones. Empathy and compassion are key in healing work but should never be used to pacify illusions, so be authentic and transparent with your experiences.

During trauma, or one of its triggers, the brain goes into alarm mode. Your ability to think and retain memory shuts off because it's not required for survival, and your brain is trying to protect you. This is why it's so darn difficult to remember the trauma itself, especially if you're being confronted by people like police officers, lawyers, or friends and family who don't want to believe you. The triggers of trauma that you acquired during your life are sometimes very unique and will quickly put your brain back into alarm mode, and you won't be able to go there. The trauma memories might not be accessible at all.

For example, if you're a survivor of repeated childhood rape, the minute your bedroom door opened, your brain was sounding the silent alarm, and your body was responding. This put you into a frozen state as the hormones triggered by your nervous system flooded your body in order to numb you. The increase in hormones disrupted the normal memory storage function. This causes flashback memories to appear—often months, years, or decades later—and on many occasions, the memories aren't intact. They are fragmented and dreamlike, and you may even observe yourself floating over the situation. As I stated earlier, out-of-body experiences are commonly reported by survivors of rape and other trauma.

Even as an adult, you may still respond to triggers with temporal dissociation, like a deer-in-headlights reaction. This isn't a fault but a normal reaction from your body to trauma or something that triggers it. You never had a chance.

Here's another memory of a trauma-induced out-of-body experience. I was in my room in my bed and suddenly realized that something wasn't right. I woke up to a voice asking me a question. I began to cry and whimper as someone asked if he'd hurt me. It was a trigger that made me sweat and realize something was very wrong.

My heart broke as I let out an ear-shattering cry of despair and turned my head to my right side—only to find myself outside of my body. I turned my head to the left, looking at a face full of pain and tears, bangs in my eyes beneath my Coke-bottle glasses, and an absolutely awry and out-of-this-world kind of feeling overcame me. At first, I didn't recognize myself, wondering for a second who the person was, until I clued in that it was in fact me.

CHAPTER 4
Getting Your Life Back

THE KEY TO RECOVERY IS to get out of the constant fight, flight, and freeze state you've been in since childhood. Pay attention to where you need to create and keep personal boundaries, so you can feel safe within your body and your home. Addictive behaviours are distractions that keep you from healing and have to be addressed and slowly worked on. The point is for your split self to learn to trust you and believe that it's safe to integrate and feel whole again, which will give you back the ability to focus, be more aware, create the life you love, and make it fully yours.

Once you abandon your state of fear, your dissociation will lift, your split psyche will merge back into one, and you'll be able to step back into your full power and lead an incredible life. Fear keeps us from real love and faith, separating us from God or our greater self. Fear is a hormonal response that becomes a program if not tackled.

Remove the program of fear and stress. Always respect yourself first. Be responsible with yourself, and union will happen.

Your first goal is to reduce any stress factors. When you feel safe and when you question your reality, your awareness will begin to increase. This means you may have to break off connections with your abusers or people who are unhealthy for you. It's wise to remove yourself from people who are abusive. Please make sure you're not exposed to people who call you names, tell you lies or untruths about your past, or otherwise hurt you. If someone makes you feel insecure or stupid, it's abuse, and you don't deserve that.

Be gentle with yourself, as you are in fact still nursing your inner child. Be soft, gentle, and encouraging toward yourself in your thoughts and out loud. Be aware of negative thoughts and how they impact your feelings and your body. Work on understanding negative thoughts, notice them, and write them down, since they can help tell a story about your past. The programming from abuse will lead to us using downgrading words and thoughts toward ourselves to keep us from healing and growing or going beyond the boundaries created to keep us trapped in suffering.

That's why it's so important to recognize the negativity directed at us. This is an illusion created through the manipulation of our minds and emotions by others, and we're the ones who continue this cycle of abuse toward ourselves that makes us believe we're bad people and unworthy of love or success. This is the lie you were made to believe, and it leads to you repeating these lies to yourself, creating the reality in which you may currently live.

We create the reality we want to live in. It's our own responsibility to create the reality we really want by shedding the old faulty program and developing a new one that serves us much better in life. Just as parents usually want to see their children succeed in life and be happy, God wants you to have an incredible life and become the best you. God doesn't want you to suffer. God wants to see you in joy and bliss, walking your life in sacred reverence. Go make your real spiritual parents proud.

Removing yourself from an uncomfortable situation may require some professional help, so make sure to talk to someone like a therapist or social worker in order to make a safe move. Remember that family and friends may not be the wisest choice to confine in.

If you feel bombarded daily by self-criticism, it may be a good first measure to try to replace them, but don't block them out completely. Be aware and observe those thoughts and know why they're there. This has nothing to do with the truth about you; it was drummed into you at some point in your childhood. When as an adult you again do something that's considered *bad* or *wrong* in your belief, those old feelings will be triggered, and this ignites the self-critical voices in your head. Aim to figure out what drove you to do something that was against your beliefs and why you carry those beliefs in the first place.

You're responsible for yourself as an adult, so be responsible enough to get help if you can't figure things out yourself. Talk therapy can work wonders. Much of this has to do with how you treat yourself. If you have little self-worth, you'll likely mistreat yourself or feel you don't deserve help or the good things in life. Mimic the positive thoughts in your behaviour toward yourself. Show yourself respect and love.

Going to a therapist for example, is an act of self-love. Writing your thoughts down will train your awareness of what's happening inside and around you. Writing is very therapeutic! It will help you feel more comfortable talking about your experiences without fear. If you can't say it, write it down.

The difficulties we face as survivors of repeated complex traumas are often derived from the notion that yet again, someone else has power over us. Even the thought of going to a therapist can be very triggering, because some of us were mistreated by so-called professionals in the past who had no idea how to handle our case and no way to understand why we couldn't speak up. Trusting a therapist or someone in authority may not be a thing we want to do.

I dealt with four therapists before I came across one I was really comfortable with and felt was able to understand me. Don't be shy to move on to something or someone else if it's not working for you or you once again feel unacknowledged. I also found that techniques related to how to help myself heal were integral to my healing journey, allowing me to feel empowered to make my own life choices. Become the observer so you can understand yourself and learn how to respond from a place of inner peace and self-sovereignty.

Find your support, such as a therapist or a good friend who can help you. Also find support for your mental, emotional, and physical well-being. If you're not feeling well overall, maybe consider taking supplements to support your brain and body during this time. In my experience, supporting my body with the nutrients that were lacking in my diet was crucial to helping myself heal from my traumas and regrow new neural pathways for new ways of thinking, behaving, and believing.

How Repressed Memories Appear

Repressed memories can be triggered just like any other memories when you think of something or experience a situation that reminds you of something from your past. However, since repressed memories are not stored in the normal places where memory is usually kept, they often need an intense emotional or traumatic trigger to resurface.

Some people never get their completed memories back. It somewhat depends on how open you are to take these on and whether or not you want to explore them. Many get back a set of memories and then shut down, stopping further investigation of even deeper hidden memories.

I think of repressed memories as areas in our brains to which there are no synapses, as if they became unplugged from the mind system. When we begin to search for our truth or recover from major trauma and our body rewires our brain patterns, those synapses may run into pockets of forgotten memories, and you'll get a dreamlike memory back out of nowhere. *Boom!* Flashback. But since you haven't touched that memory in decades, it appears dreamlike, in pieces, incomplete, or even slightly distorted. This is normal. If you're open to these memories and allow them to enter your reality, you'll find that you're retrieving more and more of them and can start to put the puzzle pieces into place.

The process happens in waves. You may not get any memories back for days, weeks, or months, until suddenly you're receiving more. Consequently, it's particularly important to keep a journal and date your experiences, describing everything as well as you can. By describing it on paper, you may be able to put the flashback to rest. If you don't express it, it will keep coming back to remind you.

It's almost like when you have something important to take care of but haven't yet discussed it with the people involved. It keeps coming up, and you can't sleep because you haven't resolved the issue. The same applies to repressed memories. Once you're going through this process, it's vital to work on it and resolve it as it bubbles up. It's now or never, and in the long run, it's very much worth your trouble. It helps you to become clear on who you are, what happened to you, and why you feel the way you do. You will finally know your story.

This awareness helps you make clear statements and establish set boundaries in your life. It dissolves dissociation. It helps to reinstate your self-sovereignty and ability to function as a well-rounded adult human being. Essentially, you're taking responsibility for your life, and I applaud you for that. You're courageous, and that's very admirable.

Each memory helps you to reintegrate a lost part of yourself, and this heals you. Recalling fragmented memories isn't something that's done *to* you, and it isn't meant to hurt you or make your life difficult. It's there *for* you and is a normal part of your healing and reintegration work to feel whole and complete again. To be honest, you were always whole and complete, and the separation was only a temporary illusion—a survival skill, as it were.

Finding Someone You Can Trust

As you start getting memories back, you may be inclined to ask family members or old friends about certain events. Until you know for sure that what you remember is exactly correct, it may be difficult to find someone to agree with your recalling of the events. You may not find anyone who can remember them or remembers them the same way you do.

Be aware that past events may look different to others due to a different perception. Your perception will never be the same as another person's. That doesn't invalidate your memory. The older the memory, the less likely you are to find someone to confirm it for you. This can become extremely frustrating, as I am sure that, just as I did, you'll try to find evidence for what you remember.

Please try not to make yourself crazy over this. It's exhausting to run around looking for a doctor or teacher you haven't talked to in thirty years. It's also likely that these people will disappoint you by saying they don't know what you're talking about, adding disbelief to your already stressed mind. Family members may also fail to confirm anything to you because they're actually involved and have tried to cover up the facts of the abuse you suffered.

Finding a close friend to talk to can be a great relief. If you get a funny feeling about this friend, however, please trust yourself and find somebody else. You're not required to keep trusting others with your memories if you don't feel 100 per cent confident that they have your back and won't abuse your trust. You're not required to keep talking. I recommend finding a licensed trauma therapist and a life coach to support you during this time.

Self-Care

Self-care and self-love are especially important for people going through this. Look at it this way: nobody ever had your back during times when you got abused. Once you know that something happened, it's time to take care of yourself and nurture your inner child. It's not selfish but an act of self-love and self-respect.

You need to come first now and take care of the wounded being that is resurfacing. Once the memories bubble up, it's your chance to take care of things for good. No more repressing it and shoving it into the bin, trying to sit on the lid to keep it down. Now is the time to do the work and look at what you've been hiding from yourself. Take your chance to do this work. After all, we always need to take care of ourselves first. We can't give from an empty cup.

Survivors and past victims of child sexual abuse tend to be people pleasers. We want others to be happy, and we want to make others happy, just like we wanted our parents to be happy or the abusers to be happy. It's not your responsibility to make others happy! What you need to learn is that happiness comes from within each person. If someone in your family is unhappy, that isn't your responsibility. You're only responsible for your own happiness and the well-being of your children or people who are in your care due to illness or disability.

Don't let others tell you that something's too much for you or that you can't handle your kids or the housework or anything else. It's very demeaning and condescending of others to proclaim that about someone else. They only do that to fuel their own ego and righteousness. They do that to put you down and feel power over you. It's a narcissistic tendency and often happens to victims of child abuse. We tend to fall into the same types of abusive relationships we'd grown accustomed to as children growing up.

If your family or spouse or friends say that about you, it's a sure sign to come home to yourself, free yourself, and remember your inner strength. You'd very likely outdo all of them if given the chance, so maybe it's time to go your own way. As a survivor of childhood abuse, you need to put your foot down and establish and maintain your personal boundaries. This can take some time to learn, but you can do it. It's important to understand your own personal boundaries—what you're okay with and what you're not okay with. You need to voice your opinion and your needs.

As survivors, we were told not to voice our opinions or talk about our feelings. Speaking up can be a huge challenge for us and very scary, but it's vital—not just for your own survival but for your healing and growth. So learn how to speak up. You can do that by taking part in speakers' groups where you can learn how to speak confidently. Alternatively, you can journal and practice talking out loud in front of a mirror until you feel more comfortable going to a speaker's event. I call this pep-talking yourself, and you can be your own best coach.

Do whatever you feel you need to do to help yourself on your healing path. Your sincere intent to heal will open doors and lead you to the places you need to experience. Be open to and aware of the signs and where your heart leads you.

CHAPTER 5

Puzzle Pieces

R ECOVERING LOST MEMORIES CAN BE compared to dropping a puzzle with a thousand pieces on the ground, then walking all over it for twenty years. Pieces get pushed into the corners of the room. Some go down the heating vents, and some are eaten by your dog. Then one day, you uncover a piece as you're remodelling your home, but you can't remember what it belongs to, so you put it on the table. Then you find another piece a little later, but it doesn't fit with the first piece, so you just put it on the table again. You keep coming across more pieces, but you'll never get the whole puzzle together—maybe 80 percent, if you're lucky.

Journaling your memories, thoughts, and feelings will help you become clearer about them and help you to realize your truth. It's a human need to make sense of things. When you can make sense of things, your world will seem less out of control. Journaling will help you bring back order into your life.

I know how expensive psychologists and therapists can be, so once you feel better, maybe only make an appointment if you feel the need to do so. Take your journaling notes and write down any questions you may have before you see your therapist, in order to make the best of your time. Write down the memories the way they appear, including the ones that feel dreamlike. You'll find a few months down the road that it will look different, because as you go along, you recover additional parts of the puzzle. Don't feel bad for not being 100 per cent accurate the first time. It's not always possible to be that precise.

Trust in the process of unfoldment. As you move along your healing path, you'll get more puzzle pieces back that will complete your life story.

Most importantly, stay open to the old memories coming back. Don't reject things just because it's initially tough to take it on or believe it. Don't shut yourself back down. Allow yourself to feel it to know that it's real. It's okay to cry. You may have a hard time expressing sadness because you've repressed it for so long and so well. You have to become comfortable again to let yourself feel it and express your emotions over your abuse and loss.

Let yourself mourn. Expressing your feelings in a healthy way will allow the healing to take place. Work with a therapist and find online support if you don't trust people in your environment. It can take a few years to complete the puzzle.

During this process, it's important to take care of your own well-being. Eat healthy organic fresh foods. Avoid alcohol and drugs or any other unhealthy substances that influence the mind and body, including cigarettes. Exercise regularly and enjoy nature. Ground your energies. I've included details of a few essential oils and their uses a little later in the book, plus information about foods that help your brain and body to perform at their peak. You need to be in your best state to get memories back, work through them, and trust yourself.

If possible, don't use crutches. If you relapse, don't punish yourself by believing that you're failing. You're not. You're doing the best you can. Be your own best support, first and foremost.

Shadow Work

A shadow is created when there's something standing in the light that casts a shadow on your life. This is about cause and effect. The light may shine straight at the thing that's casting the shadow, but if it's invisible to your mind, you won't know what it is. A shadow is anything that's become an issue in your life that you can't figure out or don't know the original cause of.

It's important for us to deal with those things that cast shadows. When we resolve the issue, there will be much more brightness and happiness in our lives. Shadows act like brake pads. They stop us from living our best life. Shadows get resolved when we take the flashlight of our own enlightenment and shine it directly at the source. Doing shadow work is incredible and means that you examine yourself and dissect parts, looking at your triggers very closely.

Understand that other people act as mirrors to you. They represent reflections of your own inner world—things that you haven't yet examined or discovered. By seeing everything around you as an aspect of your hidden self, you can easily figure out who you are and what programs are running you.

Learn from the mirrors of your surroundings. Everything is here to help you awaken. If something somebody says triggers your feelings, it triggered your ego self. Ask yourself why you were triggered and what this says about you. What attitudes, beliefs, and convictions are you carrying that made you feel triggered?

Eventually, you'll learn to escape the cycle of cause and effect when you realize that you can be the cause of change instead of suffering the effects repeatedly. Shadow work is about expanding perceptions and gaining perspective. It's the most important work you can do for yourself and your spiritual, emotional, and mental growth.

Here are some examples of shadows:

- mental blocks, feeling blocked, unable to do what others can do
- memory issues and brain fog
- lifelong depression
- unexplainable anxiety
- dissociations, also called soul loss
- clumsiness or loss of balance
- postpartum depression
- mood disorders, such as bipolar disorder
- lifelong adrenal fatigue, being tired in the morning, bags under the eyes, dry skin
- chronic lower back pain, sometimes sciatica, related to adrenal fatigue
- unexplainable chronic pain like fibromyalgia, related to adrenal fatigue
- disorders that have no known cause, like mitral valve prolapse or other issues your doctor can't explain
- eating disorders
- drug addictions or a tendency to use substances to cover up insecurities or feel better
- feeling jaded or insecure without an obvious reason
- unexplainable feelings of guilt
- feeling emotionally triggered by what others say
- no feelings for your parents or feeling uncomfortable around certain people without knowing why
- hearing strange comments from someone about the past or about your mental state
- comments about your sexual organs from a doctor that make no sense to you, like having a tilted uterus and how it's connected to women who were sexually abused as children
- unexplained scars

- comments about mental health being a family matter or that certain issues are running in the family
- your family telling you not to communicate with your cousins or members of the family with mental issues
- strangers on the street calling you by a different name
- seeing shadows flipping by at the corners of your eyes
- the feeling of something touching you when no one's there
- hormonal and skin issues that have no known or proven cause
- feeling triggered and having emotional overreactions, repressing emotions out of shame or guilt

These are only examples of my own shadows. You may have more that you'd like to add here.

Do You Report the Crime?

There will come a time when you'll feel like you should maybe take legal action. Other people may tell you to do this, but it's a personal choice. It's up to you and what you want to do.

In my case, I reported the incident to the police, or at least what I could remember at the time. I was worried about the safety of a little girl my abuser was sometimes taking care of. He was even involved in naming her, giving her the same name he gave me when he took me out to other men. Some pedophiles will take their victims to pedophile clubs or similar organizations or even sell them to other men. It was scary, so I pushed myself to report it, even though I wasn't anywhere near ready. I feared for the safety of other children, so I reported it.

Please don't have high expectations. Depending on how much time has elapsed since the last incident, and depending on where it happened and the severity of the events, there may be very lenient laws in place. It may come as a shock to you to realize that nothing will be done after you reported it. The longer you wait to contact the authorities, the less likely something will happen with your case. This is a problem because the average time it takes for survivors to recall their abuse is 37 years, as per statistics.

The reporting process is still your own choice, and you need to do what feels right to you. If you report it but nothing happens, understand that if someone else reports something about that same person, your action still may have made a significant impact. So don't shy away and think that it's

been too long. You could also provide an anonymous tip if you feel more comfortable. It may be helpful to someone else further down the road.

Aftermath

Telling your family about what you remember can be difficult and emotional. You may choose a confidant to break the news instead of doing this yourself. That's perfectly fine if you feel your confidant can speak well for you. The reaction may be backlashes, doubts, name-calling, anger, and aggression. Or they could simply ignore you.

Please make sure to have a therapist handy and on call in case you find yourself dealing with severe anxiety or a panic attack. Feeling dizzy, unwell, sick, cold; an increased heart rate; and an inability to move are all signs of an impending panic attack. If you need to, call an ambulance or ask a friend to drive you to the doctor.

There's no shame in taking medication to temporarily calm your nerves. If you're used to alternative techniques, use the one that's most comfortable to you. Later in the book, I've listed a few things that have helped me cope with panic attacks.

CHAPTER 6

What's Next?

RECOVERING MEMORIES CAN TAKE SOME time. You'll notice that they tend to come in waves, maybe once every two weeks, sometimes more or less often. Once you open the floodgate, you'll need to let it roll in until it ebbs out. This process can take up to ten years, in most cases three to four years. It depends on the severity of the abuse and the amount of time during which the abuse occurred.

At the time of writing this book, I'm still recovering occasional memories, but for the past six months there have been far fewer than there were two years ago. My abuse spanned more than nineteen years and is considered severe. The more severe the abuse, or if it's repeated abuse that you're exposed to over a long period, the more amnesia and confusion you have to deal with.

You may encounter people who'll disbelieve you because they'd always remembered the details of their own abuse. Realize that each case and each person is different, and don't let that deter you or make you feel like your memories aren't real. Being sexually abused by a parent or close caregiver is a different trauma from being sexually abused by a cousin, co-worker, friend, or other relative. It doesn't get stored the same way in your brain.

I always remembered the sexual abuse by a cousin when I was 11, although I couldn't remember all the other incidents with my caregiver. In some cases, like in child sex trafficking, you may also not remember it because you were drugged at the time, which adds another layer of confusion and amnesia. No matter what anyone else says or the nature of their experiences, trust in the way your own memories present themselves. You're unique, and so is your experience.

Medication

Medication can save your life when you're at your worst, but it should never be used over extended periods of time, as pharmaceuticals can have long-term side effects. It's something you need to consider, and when you feel you can better deal with your memories, talk to your doctor about weaning yourself off your medication and switching to alternative methods to cope with any leftover anxieties. Stay informed and learn about other self-help techniques.

As a survivor, it's important to do your own research. This gives you back your personal power and the freedom to choose your own health and wellness treatments. Contrary to what some people out there may make you believe, or you may even believe yourself, you won't have to suffer forever. Things will get better, and you absolutely will heal and recover and be able to live a beautiful life.

I know it can feel like a death sentence, but that's just your fear and anxiety telling you that. I once felt the same way. Compassion for yourself goes a long way. Put your hand on your heart and say these words:

> I acknowledge the pain and suffering I've experienced in my life and am fully aware of it. From now on, I will go through my life with love and compassion in my heart for my experiences and for those of my younger self. I herewith validate the experiences as real and will always love you and acknowledge you forever.

Repeat this whenever you have doubts or feel shame and guilt.

Look into mindfulness, meditation, supplementation, essential oils, and how you might apply this for yourself to make your life more comfortable. Learn self-care techniques. Taking quick half-hour walks every day can alleviate feelings of anxiety and depression, as can taking up a hobby like knitting or playing an instrument. If you have a dog, take half-hour fast walks with your pet and then later switch to a leisurely walk, so your dog can still enjoy a walk as well.

Essential oils have been a lifesaver to me. I make my own roller bottles with calming, grounding, and stabilizing oils, which I apply to my temples and wrists if I feel the need. I use them often even if I don't feel a need, simply to include them in my daily practices.

Essential oils affect us on the molecular level. They quickly absorb into our skin and into our cells, providing relief and healing. They're oil-based, can enter our body cells and give us healing from deep within, and stimulate our cells to function more effectively. Essential oils can also help you lift more mental and emotional blocks, as they act like keys to unlock the secrets of your mind.

Essential oils, if they are pure tested grade, can help you increase your own awareness, make better choices in life, and change how you view the world in general. Essential oils calm our emotional and mental states and help decrease the effects of fight, flight, and freeze. These oils will help you emerge from dissociative states if used regularly as a part of your wellness treatments.

Adrenal Fatigue

Adrenal fatigue is a typical condition for people who are survivors of childhood sexual abuse but may not only appear in those cases. Adrenal-fatigue patients can present with a variety of symptoms. These include constant tiredness, need for extra sleep, inability to cope with stress, reduced libido, low back pain in the kidney area or below, sighing, yawning, recurrent infections like urinary tract infections, irritability, moodiness, and cravings for sweet or salty foods. Adrenal fatigue also leads to sluggish muscles, especially in the lower back, buttocks, and legs, causing lower back pain, sciatica, and leg cramps. I had all these symptoms, and there are still days when I feel them.

There are herbal remedies that can counteract adrenal fatigue, like rosemary, basil, gingko biloba, and ginseng. It's important for you to reduce all sources of stress and anxiety, change your diet, and reduce toxins in your environment. You also need to be aware of fluoride in water and toothpaste, which calcifies your pineal gland. If you're low on iodine, similar substances like fluoride and bromine, which is found in pool chemicals, will replace the position iodine would normally take in the thyroid gland. If you don't live close to the ocean, you're likely low on iodine.

The pineal, pituitary, thyroid, and adrenal glands work together to balance your hormones and healthy brain functions. If you've experienced severe trauma, you are out of balance because of the fight, flight, and freeze response. That's why reducing toxins is particularly important, not only for survivors of trauma but also for empaths and intuitive healers who rely on a healthy functioning pineal gland.

The pineal gland, also known as the third eye chakra or the visual and auditory energy centre, assists clairvoyants with their work. It's also involved during dreaming; it releases serotonin, melatonin, and other hormones that help you reach certain sleep states and have visual dreams. During spiritual awakenings, your body will start to produce a hormone called N,N-Dimethyltryptamine (DMT). It can be naturally produced in mammals and is also called the *god hormone*.

DMT often releases when a person dies or has an out-of-body experience. Scientists studied rats and found this to be happening in some rats but not all of them. I believe this is what assists us in observing more of our repressed memories than many people believe is possible. This is still quite controversial, but I've noticed other people talking about this subject and feel it's now time to mention it.

I found some great information in a video from Joe Dispenza about the pineal gland and kundalini awakenings. Why am I mentioning this here? It's because I've had physical and spiritual experiences myself that confirm these theories. When I'm in that state, my whole body's on fire, and I have intense hot tingles all over my head, face, and shoulders. This time it's not a fear response but a response to my own superpowers having been activated. This is why I'm calling it the god hormone.

Ginkgo Biloba—The Survivor Tree

During the time when I was just two months into remembering, I had a moment of crisis. I was going through stages of awakening in a spiritual sense, and remembering trauma during such a time is quite common. Awakening comes in five stages, the first being the most difficult. I was lying there, asking spirit if I'd ever be able to deal with those memories and my past, and that's when spirit answered me.

I'm clairvoyant, meaning that spirit will often communicate with me through images. At this same time of remembering, I was also working on regaining my spiritual gifts, and so I performed the opening of the third eye to help me clear away anything that might block me from seeing. Following this little procedure, a green leaf popped into my third eye vision. It was a half-rounded leaf with a split down the middle.

I had no idea what type it was, so I googled it, literally taking my phone to look up leaves. It was a ginkgo leaf, and I conducted further searches into its meaning and history. Apparently, the ginkgo biloba was one of the few trees that survived the nuclear blast in Hiroshima in August 1945. Some 170 trees survived the atomic bombing, and each tree at the centre of the blast within a fifty-five-kilometre radius was marked with a sign that read *hibaku jumoku*, which means "survivor tree."

There are apparently 170 survivor trees representing thirty-two different species. A four-year-old ginkgo biloba sapling of one of those survivor trees was planted on August 6, 2013, in Geneva, Switzerland, on the sixty-eighth anniversary of the atomic bombing of Hiroshima.

Ginkgo biloba is used as an herbal medicine to improve memory. It's the oldest tree on Earth and has been widely studied for its effective anti-inflammatory, antioxidant, platelet-forming, and circulation-boosting effects. According to current research, ginkgo biloba benefits include improved cognitive function, improved skin conditions, positive mood, increased energy, improved memory, and reduced symptoms related to multiple chronic diseases. It's been used as a natural asthma remedy as well as a treatment for ADHD and dementia. In fact, it was believed to be so effective that in Germany, you needed a prescription for it.

Ginkgo is safe, effective, and benefits the body in numerous ways because it exerts protective effects against mitochondrial damage and oxidative stress, similar to most essential oils. It was used in ancient China especially for circulatory problems and those related to declining memory. Ginkgo contains flavonoids and terpenoids that have strong antioxidant properties. Flavonoids are plant-based antioxidants that protect the nerves, heart muscle, blood vessels, and retinas from damage. Terpenoids such as ginkgolides improve blood flow by dilating blood vessels and reducing the stickiness of platelets. The ability to improve the health of blood vessels means it supports brain activity, development, detoxifying mechanisms, and immune function.

I realized a few weeks later that the message from spirit about ginkgo biloba was designed to help me during my memory recall process, which could apparently take up to ten years to complete. I started taking it as a supplement in 2016. I feel it has greatly improved my memory and my ability to focus and stay in the present moment. It's helped me with anxiety, dissociation, and stress, and it has greatly improved my ability to work through the puzzle pieces of my childhood. It may in fact have helped me get back many more memories than I thought I'd ever be able to retrieve.

I don't know about you, but I've noticed an increase in the number of new trees planted in the area where I live. They are all ginkgos! In my town, there are three of them just steps away from my home, and there are ginkgos planted in my neighbouring town all through the downtown area. Look around, and you'll notice how our environment responds to the changes within us. As we awaken, our divine mother supports us with all we need. We only need to listen and follow her advice.

Every plant on Earth has a purpose. Nothing grows for no reason. Plants are here to support our health and our progress. It's a natural development. Everything there is carries a message or an antidote for something we need to live better and evolve.

Here are twelve proven ginkgo biloba benefits:

- increases concentration
- reduces risk of dementia and Alzheimer's
- helps fight anxiety and depression
- helps treat headaches and migraines
- fights premenstrual symptoms
- helps maintain vision and eye health
- helps prevent and treat attention deficit hyperactivity disorder
- improves libido
- lowers symptoms of asthma and asthma-related conditions
- helps heal haemorrhoids
- fights fibromyalgia
- helps reduce the effects of adrenal fatigue

As with any herbal remedy, always consult your doctor before starting to take gingko biloba to find out if it interferes with any medication you might currently be taking. Please inform yourself before deciding to take this on a regular basis. Although it's very safe, there's still a slight possibility that it could cause effects that we may not be aware of. For example, for people who take medication for high blood pressure, ginkgo biloba could potentially lower it further.

Ask a licensed holistic practitioner and your pharmacist if ginkgo biloba is safe for you. Medical doctors often don't know about the reactions between herbals, essential oils, and medications, mainly because they generally don't learn much about that in the course of their medical schooling.

I found people are often afraid of trying something different from what they've been programmed to believe in by the system that's currently in place. If it doesn't work, you have to approach things differently, since nothing can be built on obsolete building blocks. To heal, one needs to lower barriers and drop fears to welcome new inspiration. I can promise, by the grace of my own experiences, that dropping your fears will change everything you once believed was true.

Natural Remedies

Everything has a purpose, and so do plants that grow here on our Mother Earth. She provides us with all the medicines we could possibly need, just like we were born with all the skills that will help us go through life. Everything we need is already here; we just have to pay attention and ask for it. It's interesting how our divine mother will provide us with what we require. In the case of ginkgo biloba and its medicinal effects, it's intriguing how the effects benefited my ailments.

I'd suffered from bad vision all my life. As a child in first grade or possibly earlier, my vision started declining rapidly. My body had been pushed into reacting allergically to stimulants at that same age. I feel that my immune system was triggered after experiencing severe shock due to the rape. I had severe seasonal allergies and respiratory symptoms. I often find that allergic reactions can be triggered in a young child who is going through severe stress or trauma, although the sensitivity level of each person may be different.

My heart had also experienced severe stress, and ever since that time, I had heart palpitations, especially during stressful situations. At age 32, I was diagnosed with a mitral valve prolapse—a condition where a heart flap is loose and won't close properly. Other childhood rape survivors have reported heart palpitations and mitral valve prolapses as well. I believe it may relate to the weakening of the muscles due to experiencing the repeated dorsal dive effect, meaning repeated exposure to high levels of fear hormones as a child.

When we listen to our divine guidance, we can truly find what we need to help ourselves live better lives. Listen, watch, and feel for it. It's there; it's just a matter of quieting your mind, raising your own frequencies, and relearning to listen to spirit and your own higher self. Ask and you shall receive your answers.

Nutrition for Brain Health

Use oils and nutrition to aim for a healthy brain. You're going through a lot, and you need to aid your brain during this intense time. Look into nutrition that stimulates the brain and add exercise routines to stimulate your body and mind. Movement of the body, like shaking or dancing, can greatly release old trauma from your cell memory.

Look into meditation groups and emotional freedom techniques (EFT), which you can learn more about on YouTube. You can also research oils and herbals that can help brain function. I found ginkgo biloba to be a great addition to my daily vitamin routine, as it increases mental capabilities and reduces anxiety. Ginkgo promotes blood flow to the brain. Look into a whole-food multivitamin that includes ginkgo biloba. Make sure it's a good whole-food source and organic or vegan.

Our brains are made up of 60 percent fat. We need healthy fats included in our diet, such as omega 3 and omega 6 fatty acids, along with nonessential fatty acids like EPA and DHA. Our brain demands a constant supply of glucose in order to function—glucose from carbohydrates, which we can get from grains, but no refined sugars or sweets, as they only increase the risk of diabetes and obesity.

The following foods help to maintain a healthy brain:

- avocado
- beans and legumes
- blueberries
- broccoli
- chia
- dark chocolate
- nuts
- quinoa
- red cabbage
- rosemary
- spinach
- sunflower seeds
- tomatoes
- whole grains

Aim to eat more alkaline foods and drink clean, fresh, and alkaline spring water without any added chemicals, as these only lead to more issues with the brain. Acidity adds to calcification.

Essential Oils for Brain Health

How do essential oils affect the brain? They do the following:

- influence mood and emotions
- support healthy brain function

- protect neurons
- penetrate cell membranes
- protect against the effects of stress chemicals in the brain
- support neurotransmitter communication

Sesquiterpenes or plant chemicals can pass the blood brain barrier and influence positive blood flow. They are antiseptic, anti-inflammatory, can produce profound effects on emotions and hormonal balance, work on the liver, are a gland stimulant, and increase oxygen around the pineal and pituitary gland.

What Are Essential Oils?

Essential oils are the essences of healing flowers, roots, and leaves—the parts of plants that heal and smell amazing. Essential oils assist in healing you from the inside out. They can uplift your mood, calm down worried feelings, relieve stress, help with behaviour issues, increase focusing, affect memory and learning, support healthy cellular activity, and encourage healthy habits. They can also aid in restoring your immunity on a cellular level.

Essential oils contain substances from plants like linalool that help stimulate cells and encourage the metabolism to perform at its best. Overall, essential oils induce feelings of well-being and inner peace. Essential oils are the gift of our Mother Earth, here to assist and help heal us from the traumas we've suffered in life.

The question arose regarding how we can justify using tons of flowers and herbals to just create small vials of essential oils for personal use. I was curious too about how Mother Earth feels about us using essential oils for our healing. Is it not selfish? I asked her myself, and this was her answer:

> Your healing is in my best interest. If my essences allow you to heal your mind and heart, then please take from me to do so. Only a healed human being will treat me with the respect I deserve.—Mother Gaia

Here are the top suggested oils that support mental health, reduce the effects of stress, and calm emotional overwhelm:

- **Frankincense** is an amazing oil that's been used to support healthy cellular function for thousands of years. It's a wonderful mood support and improves focus and concentration.

It also reduces hyperactivity, impatience, irritability, and restlessness. Metaphysically speaking, it's an oil that's known to help resolve father issues.

- **Melissa** supports a healthy immune system, calms tension and nerves, assists with stomach discomfort, is a powerful oil for treating cold sores and warts, and is the best oil to assist trauma survivors.
- **Lavender** is calming and able to balance strong emotions, soothe skin irritations, support the cardiovascular and nervous systems, ease muscle tension in the head and neck, and act as a natural antihistamine.
- **Neroli** assists in calming anxious feelings, promotes healthy cell production, reduces inflammation, assists with mental health and clarity, and improves hormone concentration in the body.
- **Petit grain** is a calming and relaxing oil that supports a healthy immune and nervous system, promotes restful sleep, is an excellent source of antioxidants, and is known as the man's lavender.
- **Spikenard** promotes feelings of calmness and relaxation, is an excellent purifying agent for the skin, and has an uplifting aroma.
- **Copaiba** supports a healthy cardiovascular, immune, digestive, nervous, and respiratory system. When applied topically, this excellent antioxidant helps keep the skin clean and clear.
- **Peppermint** is an energizer and can be used to stimulate the mind and calm nerves, as well as help to support memory, focus, concentration, and mental performance.
- **Rosemary**, like peppermint, is an uplifting oil used to stimulate the mind and body. It can also improve cognitive performance and mood. Rosemary has been known to ease constipation and symptoms of depression and also reinvigorates appetite.
- **Bergamot** can be used to lessen anxiety, agitation, and mild depression or stress. Bergamot is mood-elevating and calming and is also used to relieve insomnia.
- **Lemon balm** can help calm and relax people who are dealing with anxiety and insomnia. It improves memory and eases indigestion.
- **Ylang-ylang** oil can help ease depression while also promoting good sleep patterns. It's a great oil for people living with Alzheimer's and is used together with inner-child work.
- **Lemon or citrus oils** are very uplifting to the mind and body, promoting physical energy and purification. Clinical studies support the use of lemon essential oil for reducing stress and boosting mood.
- **Clary sage** assists with menstrual cycle discomfort, helps balance hormones, and lifts and lightens mood.
- **Wild orange** is a powerful cleansing and purifying agent, used for digestive and immune support and skin health. It increases physical energy and elevates mood

- **Sandalwood** is known for its effects on brain health, mood, and emotional wellness. It promotes healthy skin, reduces the appearance of scar blemishes, and is frequently used in yoga and meditation for its grounding properties.
- **Chamomile** soothes skin irritations, calms emotions and the nervous system, and supports a healthy inflammatory response.
- **Basil** reduces anxious feelings, providing great benefits to both the mind and body due to its high linalool content. It's an ideal application to help reduce feelings of tension when applied to the temples and back of the neck. It's commonly used in cooking. It promotes focus and a stress-relieving experience, greatly beneficial for people experiencing adrenal fatigue.

There are many more choices when it comes to essential oils. Which ones you choose for yourself often depends on accessibility and pricing, and is basically a personal preference. The point is to help your body heal itself, not put more mind- and body-altering products into it. Give your body all it needs to fix and condition itself in order to function at its best. We call this *proactive health care.*

A number of methods of application are recommended for the brain. Aromatic diffusion involves application to pulse points on the front of the neck or wrist; the occipital point where the base of the skull and the spine meet; and the bottom of the feet. The big toe is a reflexology point for the brain. Some essential oils can be taken internally, but only if such a method is indicated on the bottle.

To obtain the full effect, it's important to find ways to incorporate oils into your life. If you're able to use them daily, the effects will be much more noticeable than if you only use them when you feel symptoms that you'd like to alleviate. You can live more symptom-free if you use the oils regularly, even if you don't feel the need for them. I use them a few times every week for a couple of hours, and overnight I run my diffuser while I sleep. I also use a few drops with my smoothie or may add a few drops to a sauce after cooking, just before serving.

I use a salt scrub that I make myself. Salt cleanses your energetic field of anything that may have become attached. It can be harsh on your shower walls but works wonders for your mood and energy. I add a couple drops of essential oils to my salt scrub and keep it in the shower. My preferred oils for the salt scrub are frankincense, patchouli, gardenia, rose, wild orange, and myrrh. I've included my recipe later in the book so you can try it out.

When choosing essential oils, it's important to do your research and make sure you're getting therapeutic-grade oils that are made using the purest ingredients, with no added chemicals or artificial scents. Use oils that are made by a reputable and professional company and have a clean, energetic imprint. It helps if they're organic and made by people who are supported by the company and treated fairly.

It's also important to follow any suggestions on the label or from the manufacturer. For example, some oils shouldn't be used internally or can be strong if applied to your skin, such as oregano, tea tree, or cassia. If you choose, you can dilute them with a carrier oil for your skin, such as fractionated coconut oil if you're not allergic to it. Essential oils seem to be more effective if diluted with a carrier oil than if you engage in pure application, according to a study conducted by one of the oil companies I know. This is most likely due to higher skin absorption rates.

CHAPTER 7

Unlocking the Secret Door

SURVIVORS, YOU ALWAYS KNEW SOMETHING wasn't right. You felt like something wasn't in order, that you were forgetting things or losing time, or that you had gone through an ordeal, but you couldn't put your finger on what that was all about. You asked your family questions, but nobody seemed to know what you were talking about.

You may have experienced symptoms such as mood disorders, dissociative states, multiple identities, depression, eating disorders, fidgeting, pulling out your hair, cutting yourself, chronic tiredness, a sensitive startle reflex, and clumsiness. You may have suffered from negative body image and low self-esteem without a clear reason why. Or maybe you've assigned a reason to your issues so you could make sense of them, but those reasons may not actually be the original reasons.

You may have experienced sexual difficulties, strange fetishes, or issues in relationships. Perhaps you've suffered from postpartum depression or had fears about having your babies taken from you—unrealistic fears of your children getting hurt or somebody abducting and hurting them. Such inexplicable fears and anxiety probably kept you up at night.

You might have experienced headaches that were severe and turned into migraines with aura. You may have suffered mini-seizures or even heart palpitations, mitral valve prolapses, or other strange illnesses and abnormalities. These may even include allergic reactions.

Everything that happens in life has a reason. There's a cause and an effect. If you have an effect but are unsure about the cause, you visit doctors, but no one can tell you why it's there or you get the excuse that it must be genetic. You may even be told that it runs in the family.

Of course, just because it runs in the family doesn't mean it's genetic. It's more likely that what happened to you typically happens to others in your family as well, so you end up exhibiting similar health problems. It could be a diet your family's practicing, or the area where you live might mean that you're exposed to specific environmental conditions. Alternatively, it could be that sexual abuse runs in your family, which is common. Because of the subject's sensitivity, it won't be talked about or addressed, simply hushed up and brushed under the carpet.

You may be told that mental illness or drug addiction is prevalent among your family members. In many cases, these family members are also victims and can't remember the abuse like you do, usually because they haven't awakened yet. They're also traumatized. The perpetrators will know what they did, but the victims won't know what happened to them.

Most perpetrators won't admit to anything and instead will question your sanity. If, like me, you've had spiritual experiences, they'll certainly use that against you as proof of your mind being unstable and that you're making things up. But experiences can't be made up. They either are or they aren't.

You may want to start looking at your life. Examine things you've been told in the past that made no sense. Consider illnesses and symptoms you've suffered that didn't have a logical explanation. Even with such an explanation, most illnesses can be traced back to a deeper underlying issue that nobody will address.

No doctor will diagnose you as a child rape survivor. I was lucky to have had three experiences with female doctors who mentioned that there was something unusual pointing toward sexual abuse in my childhood or young teenage years. At the time, as I hadn't yet retrieved my conscious memories, I rejected their hints as nonsense.

Your body and your intuition have been telling you something in a strange language you can't understand. Your body will try to get your attention because your body has needs, and as a survivor of sexual abuse, you learned to ignore your body more than others would. Your body has become your enemy, but it wants to be your friend. Your body will try to remind you of the trauma you endured with all the previously mentioned symptoms.

This may also come out in your dreams, sleep disturbances, and nightmares. The images in your mind might resemble the abuse setting or may be masked and only feel like the abuse setting, because your mind won't allow you to see it until you're ready. Your mind is very smart, functioning for you even if you don't instruct it to do so.

For example, your brain takes care of your breathing and your heartbeat, all without you making a conscious decision to take a breath or pump blood. It just happens in order to guarantee your survival. The same applies to experiences that can't be categorized by a young mind. If the mind can't categorize something, it becomes overwhelmed. To avoid this, your mind has a system in place to bypass experiences that are too difficult to comprehend. Again, this is a survival skill.

One day, you'll encounter a situation or a person that will subconsciously remind you of your childhood memories, which aren't consciously accessible to you. However, your mind will start to fire up and try to connect to those memories. This can cause déjà vu, even multiple incidents in the same day.

This is a sure sign that you're on the right track. Your mind is trying to access the hidden parts of your memory, although it's like you hit a locked door and bump off it every time you try to walk through. The door is firmly locked. You need a key to enter, meaning that you need to drop your fears and surrender. I call this *key surrender*.

You need to surrender the need to control everything with your mind and surrender to your fears of losing control. Surrendering isn't giving up, simply giving in and letting things unfold as they will. Surrendering means you relinquish control over the illusion of your reality that you'd built to protect you from your truth. If you can surrender yourself to the higher power, your higher self, spirit, God, or your true memories, you'll receive the key to open that part of your mind, the secret door, which leads to your lost memories.

Basically, you need to want to remember. You need to express that you're ready and in a safe place to relax and let go. And you need to get to a point where you can admit that you can't control everything in your life anymore. Start to trust the process of unfoldment. This is now your time to wake up and let your angels take the wheel.

Surrender is the key to your heart, the one you used to lock your heart away from all the pain that was too hard to take. You locked it and threw away the key, just like I did. When you reconnect your heart and mind, body and spirit can be reconnected. Your fragmented self and the lost soul parts can be invited to join and merge with your body, wholly and completely.

That's when you'll finally be able to understand the language your body has been speaking to you. Your heart and body will give you the feelings and impressions which your mind will receive. Connect to memories that become accessible after you've unlocked the secret door. Your mind will then be able to translate it into human language. and you'll finally be able to express your feelings and your memories, either voicing them out loud or writing them out in a journal. The key of surrender opens the gate to a miracle.

The floodgate is open. You're learning to use your voice, which had been taken from you as a victim. And so begins the process of putting your mind's puzzle pieces back together.

Surrendering is only the beginning. You'll encounter many moments in which you'll question yourself. *Am I on the right track? What if I'm wrong? Where's the proof? What if people think I'm crazy? I'm not supposed to ask this, and my parents will reject me if I go there.*

Every time you ask, you stand at a crossroads or a roadblock. You must decide to move forward. You need to allow yourself to see more and know more. Find the next key, which is allowance. Allow yourself to know your truth.

The keys to the hidden parts of your mind are as follows:

- surrendering or dropping your fear of knowing the truth
- allowing unfoldment to happen and allowing yourself to know
- connection with your inner space, or your spirit, for answers
- awareness, which you can increase and observe your memories
- acceptance that the impossible could be possible
- self-respect in terms of treating yourself well and creating boundaries
- self-love and embracing self-compassion
- self-nurturing and filling up your own cup
- self-forgiveness so you can remove the attachments to past resentments and acknowledge feelings of shame and guilt to dissolve their illusions

Fear Versus Faith

Our own fears are our worst enemy. Fear is what keeps us frozen. Fear keeps us from taking appropriate action, causes clumsiness, and takes away our voices and our minds. Fear makes our body sluggish and immobilizes us, but most of all fear breaks our connection to the infinite being of God. We're unable to hear, see, or know our own soul wisdom and reject it because of fear.

With cortisol and adrenalin racing through us, we can't go into a meditative state to access infinite wisdom. You may have noticed that as a trauma survivor, you have difficulty meditating. You may even feel triggered by people suggesting that you should be meditating. Meditation doesn't work if you're in fight, flight, and freeze mode, which has become a program due to the exposure to repeated long-term abuse.

How can you access your soul wisdom with your hormones running rampant? It's impossible, and so I emphasize the importance of reinstating peace and harmony into your life. The calmer you become, the more clearly you can hear your inner voices speak. This means you're going to have to be a little selfish. We call that self-love. You can practice self-love by creating boundaries and limitations for others, which you're going to keep at all costs. Learn to trust yourself and have faith in beneficial outcomes. You'll very soon find your way back home.

Awareness In Relationships

As a survivor, before you were aware of your past—or maybe you knew but never took a close look at it—you might never have been in therapy. You may not have had the chance to truly work through those shadows of yours, so you repeatedly found yourself in toxic relationships. Some of those relationships may have felt exceptionally good and comfortable, and you were happy. Yet one day, you may have realized that you had no control over your life or had lost your freedom, because you let the other person take you over.

It's common for survivors to marry narcissistic men. As a woman, I have a more female perspective on this, so if you're a man reading this, I apologize. We tend to attach to men who entertain us with their talk and wit. It means we don't have to talk about ourselves. We can silently play along in life and live without having to face our harsh realities.

Over time, we give ourselves amnesia and fail to notice our dissociative states. The stronger partner will often take advantage of our disassociations, along with our apparently confused and forgetful mind. They may make fun of our clumsiness when we hit our head on the freezer or break our toes when bumping into furniture.

You may suddenly realize that your partner has accused you of doing or saying things that you can't ever recall saying or doing. You may also realize your own inability to pull up those memories exactly as they were. And if you do, you find that they differ much from how your spouse remembers it. Now who's right?

At some point, if your relationship is a bit shaky—and many survivors are in that situation—he'll start to pick up on this and even begin to imply things you said, just to keep the upper hand. If you're in a state of realizing that something isn't right, you may have been triggered already by something or someone, and you're already questioning your reality. You then start to understand that what your spouse is telling you isn't always so truthful.

You start to think back, allowing yourself to recall past experiences, conversations, and anything else your partner may accuse you of. As you do that, you've just received that second key, which is allowance. You're allowing yourself to dig for your truth.

Why do we tend to move from one abusive situation to another? When one gets manipulated and groomed for many years, one gets accustomed to, and feels a certain level of comfort around, people who are manipulative and abusive. It's often very difficult to get out of that until one fully realizes the situation and its toxic effects on the mind, body, and soul. When you realize that you don't own your life anymore, that everything's about the other person and everything you say is being turned and used against you to keep you small and insecure, you're beginning your awakening journey.

This is unlikely to be well received by your partner, boyfriend, or husband, because he'll lose control over you and your life. Trust me, he'll fight that with full force. What happens next may feel like a horror story of deceit, gaslighting, and triangulation. He'll try to ruin your support system to ensure that he has power over the situation.

This is a very typical pattern that we recognize as the synergy between an empath and a narcissist. What I'm trying to show you is the importance of awareness. You need to *want* to be aware of yourself, your thoughts, your feelings, and your surroundings, along with what others are saying and when they're saying it. Aim to become a sponge for information. This will help you tune in to your awareness.

You can meditate to help you become more aware. Meditation calms us and helps us with dissociation. When you find your mind wandering, get it back. You can use candlelight to train yourself to focus your attention; just be careful with fire. But meditation is not all about calming your mind by emptying it, we calm our minds by addressing the problems that arise. In meditation, we get to explore the issues we are faced with and often receive divine guidance while in this meditative state, as long as you remember to ask your questions.

When we're calm, we don't dissociate. Dissociation happens when we get upset, when adrenaline and cortisol levels rise, or when we worry or experience something that subconsciously reminds us of our traumas. It happens when our heartbeat becomes faster. Dissociation happens whether or not we're aware of the trigger.

Your goal in becoming stronger and more aware, confident, and grounded can be found in training your awareness, meditating, and connecting deeply with yourself, your body's energy centres, and your grounding to Mother Earth. Grounding is absolutely vital for us, since we're so deep in our heads during the recovery process. You may find you've been in your head your whole life. This is so common because we didn't want to be in our bodies or our hearts. We escaped into our minds and delved into imagination and dreams to escape our reality.

Please ground every day, at least a few times. I've included some grounding techniques later in the book.

Triggers

A trigger is anything that will cause you to experience a memory or a thought—something that reminds you of your past experiences. A trigger can be a thought, emotion, or something someone says or does. A trigger can cause you to go into your past to pull up something that may or may not be disturbing. If it is disturbing and associated with the trauma in any way, you may experience a dissociated state.

While in this state, you'll find it difficult to register anything that's being said or done in the present moment. You may lose your train of thought. You may stare like a deer in the headlights. You may not be able to understand what's going on or what's being said and ask the person in front of you to repeat themselves, sometimes multiple times.

If the other person makes fun of you or pressures you for answers, this just became an abusive situation for you. The other person may or may not be aware of what's going on. If this person is aware of it and is taking advantage, you're in an abusive relationship. If not, it may simply be a misunderstanding. This is difficult to figure out from your end, and so it's often recommended to go to counselling.

People might make fun of you afterward or simply think that you're stupid. Well, you're not. You're just having a normal reaction to something that triggered a memory of a past trauma. The strangest thing is that when you get triggered, before you started to recall the events, you often react emotionally or just withdraw completely. This is because your mind doesn't allow you to see the memory but only triggers you to react or withdraw. This leaves you and others wondering over your reaction or your withdrawal to an external stimulus.

You'll feel misunderstood, but you'll also be unsure of why you reacted in such a manner. In fact, you may not even realize that your reaction wasn't normal, because that's how you've lived your entire life. It's normal to you.

What could be a trigger? First, you need to train yourself to remember what happened just before you got triggered. This can be difficult, because we dissociate and may not remember this trigger, but I want you to try anyway. Write it down if you can; keep an open notebook or use your phone's notes application. There are also apps that encrypt notes and require an access password if you're uncomfortable about others potentially reading what you've written. I recommend always keeping your phone locked with a passcode that nobody else could ever figure out.

Here are some of my triggers. It's likely that yours will be similar if you experienced sexual abuse by a parent or were subjected to child sex trafficking. Potential triggers that lead to dissociation include:

- knocking on the door
- sudden opening of a door
- sudden appearance of a person
- having to explain yourself to a male, such as in a job interview
- being touched inappropriately
- being touched or hugged
- eating food
- thinking of something disturbing
- watching a show about a trauma experienced by a child
- loud voices
- severe guilty feelings
- someone wanting to hold your baby
- engaging in sex
- someone trying to bully you
- having to speak up, especially if you were always told to let others speak for you or not to open your mouth
- someone interrupting your thought process
- being home, particularly if you always feel drawn to go for drives or otherwise stay away from home
- scents such as cigar smoke, alcohol, or aftershave

There are many more possible triggers, including a certain tone of voice, having to be alone at night, or people touching your toes (for example, if you were tortured).

Before you remembered the events, these triggers caused you to dissociate so you wouldn't remember the actual trauma. However, when you have the key to the parts of your mind you forgot, and you have learned to be more observant regarding your memories, thoughts, and feelings, you'll start to access those memories after being triggered instead of dissociating. This could happen immediately after the trigger occurs, but with old trauma, it's more likely to reappear days or weeks later. I usually recalled the memories hours, days, or weeks after I got triggered, so it was even more complicated to figure out a specific trigger for a memory. This is why it's especially important to keep a journal.

Dissociation is also known in the spiritual community as *soul flight*. You're dislodging from yourself during an unpleasant experience. It usually happens with the increase of hormones in the body—adrenaline and cortisol, for example—when the body goes into a fight, flight, or freeze response. When your body experiences this more often than normal, you can develop adrenal fatigue.

Adrenal fatigue isn't frequently discussed in the medical community. It's essentially an array of symptoms potentially caused by an increase in hormonal release of the adrenal glands, which leads to the adrenals becoming exhausted over an extended period. The pituitary gland will then produce a hormone to try stimulating the adrenals to produce cortisol. This can lead to chronic fatigue and depression.

Memories of old trauma appear often in a dreamlike manner at first, so we often push them away. As children, we were told that we must be dreaming or that we have an overactive imagination in order to keep us quiet. The following are some of the most common symptoms of adrenal fatigue:

- difficulty getting up in the morning
- high levels of fatigue each day, mainly in the morning
- inability to handle stress
- cravings for salty and sweet foods
- higher energy levels in the evening
- overuse of stimulants like caffeine
- a weak immune system

- asthma, allergies, or respiratory issues
- dark circles under the eyes
- dizziness and fainting spells
- depression and anxiety
- dry skin, particularly on the legs, or adult acne
- extreme tiredness an hour after exercise
- frequent urination
- insomnia
- joint pain
- lines in your fingertips, and decreased collagen making fingerprints appear fainter
- loss of muscle tone
- low blood pressure
- low blood sugar
- low sex drive
- lower back pain
- numbness in your fingers, poor circulation, or waking up and not feeling your limbs
- weight gain, which some of us counteract with bulimia

I had all these symptoms, and all my doctor had to offer was an antidepressant. At the time, I was pregnant and intuitively refused the pharmaceutical drug. I knew there was more to my situation, and I wanted to find out.

Adrenal fatigue is a stress-related condition that results in symptoms like exhaustion, weakened immunity, sleep disturbances, and food cravings. The adrenal glands and HPA (hypothalamic-pituitary-adrenal) axis become depleted, especially following a long period of emotional stress or chronic illness. You can counteract these effects by improving your diet, engaging in mind-body exercises, taking the right supplements, removing stress, and getting better sleep. Basil is an amazing herbal remedy for adrenal glands and stress. It can support you on this journey and is delicious in salads, teas, or sauces.

How do you figure out you're a trauma victim if you can't remember it? Well, there's no one way to know until you remember at least some of it, but doctors often look at the whole picture to see if what you think happened fits the setting. If it doesn't exactly follow a pattern, don't be discouraged. Your memory will return more and more if you invest in your own self-care and learn to reconnect with yourself on a deeper and more intimate level.

Some of the patterns that fit the bill may be a mother who's overly particular about cleanliness and portraying the perfect family image, or depressed parents who may appear all happy and positive when outside of the home. Maybe it's a family that on the surface is well put together—perhaps business owners with Mom staying home with the kids most of the time or they have a home-based business. The kids have no voice in anything at home; parents speak for the children. The kids' rooms look perfectly kept, with pictures and posters on the walls covering up most of the free space. Posters may serve as a visual distraction during times of trauma or also as something to identify with. Constantly preoccupied or busy with something, the mother never plays with the children or seems to have a disconnected emotional bond with the kids, acting more like a nanny than a mom.

A different image is presented outside of the home than what it's really like within those four walls. You don't feel like it's safe to be open about your feelings with your parents or even your siblings. Issues with health may occur—for example, stress symptoms like loss of hair. Your parents may say things that make no sense to you. Friends may tell you that your home is so quiet you could hear a pin drop. The home decor often has a sterile look, in grey or faded colours. Your mother may tell you not to bring other kids home for playing, overly concerned about what other people might think or say.

Other factors might be a father who stays out a lot or for a long time, or one parent might give you gifts while the other withholds things. Being told to leave old things in the past is also a common occurrence. There may be drug and alcohol or prescription drug abuse running in the family. Some uncles may also be involved in abusing their kids or you during family gatherings. Nothing is ever obvious, but you may hear things from friends or even strangers that your family is known to contain child molesters. You may be told to stay away from certain family members without being given a clear reason.

Child abusers can be very vigilant and amazing at cover-up and brainwashing techniques because they teach each other. Over years and decades, these strategies are passed on from one abuser to another in clubs and at social gatherings. They pretend it's a family gathering or a club of sorts, and trust me, you wouldn't know that there was more to it.

When I was a child, the internet was limited, so clubs were created with specific symbols that would only be recognized by child molesters, like going to a nightclub or a red-light district. They had special markings on places where they sold children for sex. You could see it online on their websites, on the bottom of the pages, or somehow hidden in the titles, text, or pictures. Today, abusers can easily prey on kids online and go to great lengths to make the most of it.

In my childhood days, we were told not to talk to strangers and to stay away from the road if a car pulled up. Today, people often don't let kids walk around alone like they did when I was young. These days, abusers go online and befriend your children on social media, then end up coercing children into meeting up or sending pictures of themselves. If you've ever visited an online dating site, you'll know exactly how they do it. The abusers use the same methods with kids on Instagram that they use on dating sites with adults. There's no real difference, except in some of the language they employ to coerce someone. You can easily be preyed upon as an adult, so just imagine how the situation might unfold online with an unsupervised child.

I was shocked the first time my daughter was stalked. She was on a kids' gaming app when she got messages from someone pretending to be a child her age. She called out to ask me what town we lived in. I ran over and took the game away. I sat down with her and explained the dangers of talking to strangers online. She was only eight at the time and was crying and felt horrible, realizing the danger she had been exposed to.

I'm glad we had that experience so she could understand the dangers of online games and messaging. An innocent game can be a big attraction for these people. If your child gives out information like that, you can't feel safe anymore.

The Dorsal Dive

When a person experiences severe trauma, the soul or psyche can get fragmented or split. It will feel as if you're watching yourself undergoing a certain experience, rather than going through it inside your body. This is an out-of-body experience.

The first time I was raped, I was about 5 years old. He'd tried it before a few times, but he didn't fit. He used spoons and other kitchen utensils to widen my vagina so that "I can fit one day." This made me develop a strange fetish for kitchen utensils. Until I had my memories back, I had no idea why I had this fetish.

I'm going to share one of my first memories with you—the one that kept me from speaking up for an awfully long time. It was a near-death experience that happened during the first rape. At the time, I didn't remember the rape, only the part where I dislodged from my body and found myself up on the ceiling, watching the whole thing with a bird's-eye view. I'm going to tell you about the events that led up to this. It may be graphic and triggering to you, so if you'd rather not read it, please skip ahead.

It was dark, but there was some light coming in from my door, which was propped open slightly. He was visiting me again that night. I was very sleepy when I suddenly felt I was being squished, and my legs had been spread so far to the side that it was hurting. My hands were on my chest and his body pressed on top of me, holding my hands in place.

It was dark, and I couldn't see anything. I had trouble breathing. I felt I was going to get smothered, and it scared me. He was talking to me to calm me down when I suddenly felt a burning pain in my vaginal area. As a child, I didn't really understand what was hurting me, only that this pain grew in strength and that it felt like fire. I was holding my breath, trying not to move out of fear it was going to hurt even more. I felt a burning log going up inside the length of my body, pushing against my lungs and heart.

Then it stopped. I don't remember crying or screaming. My air was taken, and I was suffocating under the weight of his body. The log retracted, and I thought for a second that it was over, feeling relieved. But I was wrong. The pain returned as he once more thrust himself slowly back into me. The burning was even more intense, and I felt panic rising inside of me. The realization hit me that it wasn't going to stop anytime soon.

He kept going, and he kept getting faster. The pain was intense, as if I were burning up from the inside out. The hot burning log filled my small body and took my breath until I suddenly felt something inside my chest. It was my heart, but it felt like a galloping horse had just stumbled and fell on my chest. My soul was screaming for it to stop.

Then I popped out of my body. Suddenly, I appeared on the ceiling of my room, where I turned around and watched. I moved my spirit back down to face my murderer, because I believed I'd died. I looked into his eyes, which were grey and glassy. His mouth was o-shaped, and his chin and upper lip were covered with facial hair. The scene looked frozen in time. I was screaming at him, telling him to stop, that he was killing me, but he couldn't hear me. He was in a daze.

I was certain that I was dead. I have memories of going to the other side and communicating with spirit and angels before I returned. I was given a guardian angel to protect me but also to help me with my life's purpose. I won't go into the details about that experience here. When I was back in my body, I was being whisked out of my bed by my mother. She sat me on the toilet. My body was numb. I couldn't feel anything from my belly button down to my knees. I wasn't allowed to look inside the toilet, but I caught a glimpse. It was black with blood.

It took me three years to get the completed memories back. I could never recall what had happened after the near-death experience. That took some time to recover. I had asked God to show me, but my mind just wasn't ready to see it until I was about three years into the process of recovering my memories.

In a situation that may appear life-threatening, you have the choice to fight, which you often can't do as a child. You can also flee, but it's often too late by the time you realize that your abuser isn't there to sing you a lullaby. Or you can freeze. When a gazelle runs from a lion and the lion catches up to it, the gazelle will stop and freeze. Its only chance to get away is to play dead. In the case of the gazelle, it's usually the end of the line. In a sexual attack, such an action may save you from experiencing rape, and it may prevent you from getting killed afterward.

Basically, your body goes into a shock. Your mind and body become flooded with hormones that will numb your experience, such as adrenalin and cortisol, the adrenal hormones. This adds to you being unable to recall the exact happenings of that moment. As it numbs the experience and you faint, it also significantly decreases your ability to recall what happened. After experiencing the dorsal dive repeatedly, together with grooming behaviours, you eventually learn to "auto faint" the minute your abuser activates your trigger to do so. This could be represented by something as simple as one specific sentence or a certain knock on the door.

Perhaps you've wondered why you can remember so much of the abuse but not the attack or the attacker's face, appearance, or words spoken. Perhaps you can only recall waking up during or after, dishevelled or with your abuser lying on top of you. This is because every time you heard that knock on your bedroom door in the middle of the night, or your abuser opened the door and peered in, you dissociated or even fainted. You won't ever be able to recall those details because you were basically passed out from the freeze response your body went into.

If you're repeatedly exposed to abuse, your body will be trained to behave like that the moment your abuser prepares to come and abuse you again. A sentence like "Your daddy needs you" might be enough for your body to immediately go into that state. You had no chance. This immediate fainting reaction is something we call the *dorsal dive*, in which you just go under. It no longer only activates during fear of imminent death but because you'd been groomed by the abuser early on, most likely as a baby or toddler. This has now become an automatic trained response within your nervous system.

Child molesters are very aware of this, and it's exactly their strategy: to groom you into this behaviour to satisfy their own needs. This ensures that they never get caught or always have the upper hand, because people will ask you how it happened or how he approached you. They will ask you to explain the process, at least in terms of what he said and did. That's where you'll lose your train of thought; you can't explain it either. And that's when the abuser will say that you're making it all up.

This was my experience as a teenager. I even went to the police but kept being picked up by my abusers because I just couldn't stand the questioning and voice my truth. I froze. I simply had no words and no understanding of the process to explain what happened at that age. Basically, the abusers not only took our bodies, hearts, and minds but also our voices. We were true slaves to our abusers and the human mind's system and organizations.

The Amygdala

The amygdala is one of two almond-shaped groups of nuclei located deep and medially within the temporal lobes of the brain. In humans and complex vertebrates, it performs a primary role in the processing of memory, decision-making, and emotional responses. It's where emotional memories get stored, like the ones related to intense fear.

The amygdalae are considered to be part of the limbic system. This system supports a variety of functions, including emotion, behaviours, motivation, and long-term memory. It also supports olfaction, a chemoreception that forms the sense of smell and is one of the reasons essential oils are so incredible for trauma healing. Emotional life is mainly housed in the limbic system and has a great deal to do with the formation of memories. The amygdalae perform major roles in the formation and storage of memories associated with emotional events, such as trauma memories.

During fear conditioning, sensory stimuli reach the amygdalae, particularly the lateral nuclei, where they form associations with memories of the event. Damage to the amygdalae, which can occur in psychosurgery, causes an interference with memory that's strengthened by emotion. I've once read about a study that had determined that a patient with bilateral degeneration of the amygdalae had poorer recollection of a violent story than a patient with functional amygdalae, indicating that the amygdalae stores connections with emotional learning.

In psychosurgery, a part connecting the amygdalae and brain stem is removed using either surgical procedures or gamma or infrared rays. This causes the patient to have fewer emotional reactions to memories of severe trauma. This type of surgery was once performed on people with schizophrenia and bipolar disorder who were deemed untreatable. I'm unsure whether it's still being used today and in which countries, although I read that the procedure had been discontinued at some point because of poor regulations that created immense controversies regarding the procedure.

Post-procedure, this surgery can cause a person to lose interest in hobbies and in life in general. I believe this procedure was applied in some cases involving child sex-trafficking victims. The procedure would be done off the record and after hours, in secrecy.

Buddhist monks who conduct compassion meditation have been shown to change their amygdalae during their practice. In an MRI study, more intensive activity was found in expert meditators than in novices. Increased activity in the amygdalae following compassion-oriented meditation may contribute to social connectedness.

To me, this shows that meditation can help make a difference for people who have experienced trauma, surgery, and an associated loss of memory, compassion, or interest in life. Alternative techniques like meditation can potentially help you to fix the effects of this procedure if you feel you may have been a victim.

We connect with others with our hearts. The heart is the gateway to establish lost connections—with yourself, your environment, people, and God. Your intent to heal yourself is all that's required for the wheels of fate to move into gear.

Other Manipulation Methods

I need to make you aware of a few more methods abusers may have used to force you to comply or to confuse you while you're being abused. One is hypnosis. This can be extremely effective in helping people to stop smoking, and it can also help with allergies or nightmares. When I was having severe stomach pains as a child, hypnosis was employed to get rid of the discomfort. My abuser was very fascinated by this method, and sure enough, he bought a book to teach himself hypnosis using a pendulum. He only did this so that he could imply things into my subconscious to confuse me and try to conceal his crimes.

It's known that people suffering from dissociation are much more prone to be hypnotized. The effects exert a greater hold on them than on a person who doesn't have dissociation as a result of complex childhood trauma. It's just another method that may have been applied. If it happened to me, it's not far-fetched to think that it happened to others as well.

The other method I need to discuss is drugs. In child sex-trafficking cases, it was especially common to use what we know as the date-rape drug called *ketamine*. It's also known as Special K, Vitamin K, or Kit Kat. There may be other names, but those were the ones commonly used in the eighties and nineties. It was used on children because it was believed that it didn't affect the pulmonary system as much as other drugs. If you passed out, there was a danger that you'd stop breathing, but ketamine was not thought to affect the breathing as severely. Consequently, it was deemed to be safer to use on children than other drugs.

Ketamine makes you hallucinate, and it numbs pain, so it was considered to be an ideal child-rape drug by pedophile rapists and their organizations. It's also one of the reasons you may have some really strange dreamlike or out-of-body experiences. If you receive one of these memories back, it will be difficult to trust yourself, and you may feel like you're losing your mind. You're not. You were simply drugged as a child, and the memory of it now appears dreamlike and distorted.

You may not have known you were drugged, as the abuser may have hidden the material in a drink, for example. Ketamine is a white powder that may come in tablet form. Sometimes it's mixed into a drink, usually cola or something similarly dark in colour, and at other times it's given as a pill or tablet. Your abuser may have claimed it was your vitamins.

The long-term effects are headaches, stomach aches, irritability, dissociative behaviour, guilty behaviour or jadedness, low self-esteem, loss of weight, and dry skin. With overuse, you may run the risk of falling into a coma at some point. It is also highly addictive. For a child, this can have severe effects.

A child or teenager can get into trouble in school due to dissociative behaviour, and the child may not be able to focus on schoolwork. This means that you may have had to switch schools or repeat a year, take extra after-school lessons, or even been a drop out. It can also lead to later issues with drugs and substance abuse.

Another method that I know of that could have been applied is the use of memory-wiping pharmaceuticals in combination with hypnosis. This may sound very controversial, but they're sometimes using these drugs to stop people from panicking after experiencing severe trauma. I came across a report on Google Scholar detailing the case of a doctor who administered a drug during surgery. A woman was able to hear his conversation with another doctor over speakerphone in the operating room, discussing her cancer and that she wouldn't live more than a few months.

She was hysterical, so he administered this drug. Shortly after, she was as happy as a peach and no longer recalling what he'd said about her medical condition.

Any form of changing a person's memory or perspectives with forceful methods, deceit, or grooming is considered manipulation. This can cause long-term mental and emotional problems for the victim further down the road. This is abuse of power.

During a time when I suddenly remembered some of my traumas at age 15, I was taken to a place where they were going to treat me, to "help me." I remember that it involved hypnosis, but I also remember that they wanted me to take a medication, which I refused to take. I'm still uncertain about exactly what happened that day, but I'm sure that one day I'll be able to recall more of those events. All I know is that when I returned home, I was calm and collected.

One of my memories was me panicking after I realized that they wanted to make me forget something, as I overheard a conversation at the dinner table. My abuser also mentioned to his partner later that he wanted to forget too and was considering doing the procedure on himself. His partner said that she'd never let people mess with her head, claiming that it was brainwashing and scared her.

I'm only telling you this because I want people to be aware of possible methods that could be applied. I have absolutely zero proof of this and am still hoping that somebody will come forward one day and admit to it or explain this all to me. But that will most likely never come to pass.

Learning to accept the possibility that one will never receive an apology, confession, validation or some sort of confirmation from the abusers or bystanders will allow one to surrender to the now. This releases the binding thoughts and wishes so we can move on and live a better life without all the constraints of the hold that past traumas have on our being. Sometimes justice is a form of revenge, but it often only leads to more pain and more karmic patterns to be resolved later on in our lives. I felt that I wanted to be free now instead.

Denial

Denial is not a river in Egypt. It's a serious condition that won't allow you to accept the truth. Researchers in Norway have discovered a mechanism that the brain uses to filter out distracting thoughts in order to focus on a single piece of information. This could explain how denial works.

When I started to remember some of the horrible things that my abusers did to me, my first question was how a mother could stand by or know about this and do nothing. It puzzled me, and I had issues believing myself because I knew I'd never be able to let someone do anything like that to my children. I'm a roaring lioness who would fiercely protect them and move away from the abuser with my children.

However, it's much more complicated than that, especially if your mother or the partner of the abuser was already living in denial. It may have started in her infancy. Victims of childhood abuse often develop a mechanism that makes them ignore obvious signs and symptoms, living like this for decades. They may never clue in to it, and if they do, their own guilt and shame will keep them from wanting to discuss the issue. They often feel very ashamed regarding their inability to protect their children, but in many instances, they don't have the means to support themselves and their children in case of a divorce. The abuser will use all this to his advantage.

When I did some online research about this, I found a great article that showed a typical conversation between a mother and a daughter, where the mother knew about the abuse and the daughter tried to tell her what was going on. Reading this conversation made me realize how it was possible. It was exactly how conversations had gone between me and my mother. I'm not going to write this conversation here to spare you the reaction I experienced after reading it myself.

The realization hit me hard. I had to stop reading the article, as I was having an intense anxiety attack. It felt as if someone had unzipped the cocoon I'd built around myself over decades, and I suddenly found myself exposed to cold air. I was going into shock. My extremities went cold, my breathing became shallow, and I started crying intermittently.

I was immediately put back into a moment when I experienced this realization as a child of maybe 10 or 12 years old. I was left in my room to cry it out and never had help. I was lying there, unable to move. At this point, I asked the angels to please protect me and the cocoon enveloped me, locking out all the unpleasant realizations. I had a panic attack and shut myself off.

But on that day when I went online and read about the denial of a mother regarding child sexual abuse, the cocoon came down. Two hours later, a friend had taken me to a hospital. I was back home that night with an anxiety medication in my bag. This was also the time when I started to investigate essential oils.

Two months later, I was weaning myself off the pharmaceuticals, as I'd found a way to use essential oils to deal with my anxiety. Since I've been using the oils, I haven't had to use any further medication. I use essential oils almost every day of my life, even replacing some toxic household items by making them myself using essential oils. When I felt anxiety creep in, I simply diffused calming oils and applied them to my wrists and behind my ears and neck, listened to meditative music and just relaxed. The anxiety subsided, and I never experienced another panic attack like that again.

The oils saved my life and my sanity. Using them consistently in various ways really made a huge difference in my overall long-term health.

PTSD AND CPTSD

Post-traumatic stress disorder (PTSD) isn't an illness but a disorder of the mind. Your brain had to adapt to the tremendous amount of stress and trauma it suffered. This is a completely normal reaction to a totally abnormal amount of bullshit you had to endure. The only way to change this is to reorder it by means of compassionate self-work.

Some mental health professionals make the distinction between a diagnosis of PTSD and complex PTSD (C-PTSD). The symptoms of PTSD mostly apply to people who have experienced a short-lived traumatic event, like a motor-vehicle accident, natural disaster, or rape. However, such symptoms aren't always as applicable to people who have experienced chronic, repeated, or long-lasting traumatic events like childhood sexual or physical abuse, domestic violence, or captivity, such as being held in a prisoner of war or concentration camp. In these instances, PTSD doesn't really seem to accurately describe the psychological harm, emotional problems, and changes in how people view themselves and the world following chronic traumatic exposure.

Therefore, some mental health professionals believe that we should distinguish between the types of PTSD that develop from chronic, long-lasting traumatic events and PTSD that is caused by short-lived incidents. The diagnosis of C-PTSD refers to the set of symptoms that commonly follow exposure to a chronic traumatic event, like sexual abuse and grooming over many years of your childhood, for example.

The traumatic events connected to C-PTSD are long-lasting and generally involve some form of physical or emotional captivity, such as childhood sexual or physical abuse or domestic violence. In these types of events, a victim is under the control of another person through coercion and doesn't have the ability to escape. This leads to the victim becoming programmed to be afraid and the hormone system to constantly respond. You're constantly in fear mode. If you've lived like this since childhood, you may have never known the difference, and your fear mode has become your normal state of being.

I've described in previous chapters how that looks in life. In my case, I always felt as though I had no self-esteem. I couldn't speak up for myself, couldn't understand social concepts, felt mentally and emotionally blocked, and was constantly hiding my feelings. I was afraid of showing my true authentic being and lived in hiding my whole life—until the day of my awakening.

The following symptoms of C-PTSD stem from exposure to a chronic traumatic event where a person felt captive. The material is partially derived from online sources that resonated with my own experiences, one of those articles I read was "An Overview of Complex PTSD" by Matthew Tull, PhD.

- **Emotional regulatory problems:** People with C-PTSD have difficulty managing their emotions. They may experience severe depression, thoughts of suicide, or have difficulty controlling their anger.
- **Changes in consciousness:** Following exposure to a chronic traumatic event, a person may repress memories of the event, experiencing flashbacks or dissociation.
- **Changes in how people view themselves:** Symptoms in this category include helplessness, shame, guilt, or feeling detached and different from others.
- **Changes in how the victim views the perpetrator:** People with C-PTSD may feel like they have no power over the perpetrator, who has complete power in a relationship. In C-PTSD, people might also become preoccupied with their relationship with the perpetrator and have constant thoughts of wanting revenge.
- **Changes in personal relationships:** These symptoms include problems with relationships, such as isolating oneself or being distrustful of others. Note that this is unique from borderline personality disorder (BPD) in that people with C-PTSD will often alienate themselves. This differs from people with BPD, who engage in unstable relationships that can be dramatic and volatile.

I believe that medication isn't a good choice for people recovering from old complex trauma. Medication changes your receptors, nerve pathways, and the chemical reactions in your body.

During the first few months of my awakening, I experienced what one might call psychological issues, including déjà vu and loss of sense of self, de-realizations, and de-personalizations. I felt like I was losing myself. I asked God or my greater self what I could do or should do to help myself. Did I have to take medication to fix things?

The answer I received was very clear and kept repeating down the road: *Don't do anything at all. Release all toxicity and let yourself heal naturally. Your body is designed to heal and accustom to the new circumstances. Give it time, give it time, give it time.*

The best way of dealing with these issues is to support your body, mind, heart, and spirit with your own compassion, self-realization, and particles in plants and oils that support cell proliferation and energy production, so your body's cells can work at their best to support your healing. This may be the longer route, but it's essentially the better one.

In my opinion, medication is meant as a temporary help if you have no other options, but the real help comes from the work you do on yourself. Learn to become a master of your thoughts and emotions, not to control them but to understand them. Once you know why you have overreactions and certain repetitive thoughts, you no longer need to control yourself, as you're growing into your own sovereignty.

Recovering old memories and putting the puzzle of your life story together is an essential and fundamental aspect of ascension. Without this work, ascension becomes a struggle and fails. Resolving the inner deeper issues that are hiding in your subconscious is therefore an incredibly important part of your soul's growth and advancement. It's inevitable. You either do it and grow or you stumble and stay behind, burying everything again and drowning in human addictions until the next chance to ascend may present itself. My suggestion is to do it now.

Please be aware that substances that change your mind—like alcohol, tobacco, and street drugs— also adversely affect your state of mind, your physical health, and your emotional and mental health. They don't help you. These are substances we get addicted to through the programming of the human mind system. They systematically decrease our ability to function at our best.

You can't heal if you keep putting toxins into your body that will artificially alter your mind and state of consciousness. Your mind was already altered. Now it's time to fix it. Your mind or brain has the capability to heal itself, with the ability to regrow nerves and construct new neural pathways, all orchestrated by you and your intent to do so.

On top of that, being under the influence of substances can decrease your credibility. Others may not trust you if you aren't sober, which can be detrimental. It's already hard enough to get others to believe your incredible story of survival. For your own sake, get off everything or get help to become sober and substance-free. There are therapies out there that can assist you, like dialectical behaviour therapy, cognitive behavioural therapy, and mindfulness. That together with using Mother Earth's treasures of essential oils, energy healing, chakra balancing, and grounding meditations can make a tremendous difference in your life.

Changes in How One Views the World

People exposed to chronic or repeated traumatic events may lose faith in humanity or have a sense of hopelessness about the future. How can one create a life of beauty and joy if one feels hopeless all the time? I began to stop watching the news and social media for some time when I noticed how my worldview was even more influenced by the negativity I was seeing on the screen. Coming home to yourself and removing manipulative mind methods online or from other people is critical in recovery from childhood trauma. Do yourself this favour and stay away from the mainstream for a while. Instead, invest time in spending precious moments with positive and supportive people if you feel like socializing.

I began to pay attention to how people are manipulated by what they watch on TV or read in the news. Every fragment of information, if taken on, has the power to change your perspective. Be diligently aware of that type of manipulation coming from the media that you're exposed to. If it doesn't personally resonate with you, it may either not be true or it may just not be your own experience.

One night, I watched a show online and felt appalled by how it portrayed fear. In the show, a group of teens summoned a demon to help steal some items for them. The demon was explaining to the teens that fear isn't something to reject; it actually assists humans in keeping them safe and stopping them from making stupid decisions. It was just a TV show, but these types of messages can become deeply ingrained in people's minds.

In fact, fear doesn't stop you from running out into the road; your awareness does. Your awareness that it's not smart to just run out on the road will stop you, not your fear. Your fear of that bee chasing you may in fact make you run into the road, where you might get hit by a car.

Fear doesn't stop me from jumping off a bridge when I have depression. My awareness does. It tells me that there's more beyond this current moment of suffering and that the experience will lead to me becoming a wiser person. It tells me I'll grow from the pain and suffering into a survivor and someone who thrives. It tells me that jumping off the bridge may or may not kill me, but it will definitely show me that I'm rejecting the greatest gift ever handed to me, which is life.

Fear states lead to dissociation, as we've already learned. Fear states lead to us not thinking clearly and not perceiving what's behind the repeating thoughts and heavy emotions we may be experiencing at the moment. Fear triggers us into an overreaction that's not always necessary. Most of our fear responses are completely inaccurate and impulsive, making us reactive and not able to respond appropriately.

Pausing before responding will often help us gain greater perspective and take appropriate action instead of a thoughtless reaction. Many people react or withhold themselves. They don't take the correct actions or don't speak up because of the fears they carry. They believe it protects them, but it actually traps them. Fear doesn't keep us safe; it keeps us trapped. Greater awareness allows us to help ourselves and others more effectively. Awareness is the key to freedom.

Every time you have a fearful thought, pause for a minute and ask yourself from where this originates. How did you acquire this idea and fearful thinking, and how do you feel you can change this state of being?

CHAPTER 8

Healthy Mind

TO KEEP YOUR MIND HEALTHY, learn the best ways to manage stress and negativity in your life, say no to responsibilities that overwhelm you, or find a way to simplify them. Understand your triggers, which are unique to you. There's no one size fits all. Make sure your spouse knows about them and helps you to reduce them.

As I mentioned earlier, you can help your body and mind by eating healthy. Include vegetables and fruits in your diet to make sure you receive all the nutrients needed by your mind, not just your body. Include healthy supplements in sensible doses if you feel you need to. Make sure they're sourced from a reputable company with a good track record and are whole-food supplements and substances that promote health, but specifically brain and adrenal health.

And finally, write. Journal every day for a while, but don't exceed the two-hour limit. We don't want to dwell in our past and emotions for too long. If it's very intense, only write for ten to fifteen minutes a day. Skip a few days if you feel anxious, since the point is for you to heal, not overexert yourself.

Remember, you're still human and have a life. Take part in healthy activities, but stay away from things that could hurt your remembering process or give you more anxiety later. Avoid drug and alcohol use at all costs, as these can have detrimental effects on a stressed mind. Find healthy alternatives like swimming, walking, socializing with friends who are supportive and uplifting, and so forth. Find what works for you.

The Effects of Caffeine

During the stressful time of recovering memories, coffee can affect you. It can catalyze an anxiety attack and contribute to heart palpitations, sweating, and shaking. It also affects your adrenal health if you consume it to excess. Your body was in the fight, flight, and freeze response for a long time, and so your system reacts more often in that manner than it does for others who haven't experienced severe repeated trauma.

Your adrenal glands run on empty a lot, and coffee will trigger them to produce more cortisol and adrenalin. This will trigger your pituitary gland to produce even more hormones to try to kick-start the adrenals' empty stores. In turn, your skin will have issues, such as breakouts, acne, or skin spots, which you may find mainly on your face, scalp, and neck. This has been my own personal experience.

It's beneficial for you to reduce your coffee intake to less than one cup a day, or try replacing it with a cup of tea of your choice. I often use essential oils to wake me up in the morning—like peppermint, basil, and rosemary—and find pleasure in consuming herbal teas. Find something you really love so that it's easier to make a switch. Keep your oils handy in your purse or in your coat so you can easily reach for them if you need a wake-up call.

Panic Attacks

If you feel you need to use pharmaceuticals to deal with panic attacks, that's totally your choice. I've used them myself temporarily, but I found that they stopped me from experiencing my emotions the way I should have. This was a vital part of my healing—realizing the reality of the memories and that my memory was actually correct.

Consequently, I don't promote pharmaceuticals, but I also don't recommend not taking them if you feel you need to or if your doctor tells you that you should. Keep in mind that if you have children, they need you, so do the right thing for the ones in your care and be responsible with yourself. Be the adult you never had in your life when you were a child.

Here are a few alternative ways to deal with panic attacks.

- daily thirty-minute fast walks
- knitting or another calming hobby

- mindfulness, bringing yourself back into the moment
- grounding techniques
- meditative music or guided meditation, free on YouTube
- reiki, which is a spiritual-awakening and self-healing tool
- qigong, for energy clearing, grounding, centering, and inner peace
- calming essential oils, diffused and applied
- drinking plenty of live and chemical-free water, such as spring water (you can add a drop of lemon oil to make it taste better if you don't like water)
- circular or square breathing
- focusing on things in the room to realize that you're safe in the moment (if you're not safe, immediately move yourself to safety and contact the police)
- living foods (raw vegan), which increase biophotons and have a calming effect
- whole food supplements to support your whole system, including mental, emotional, and physical well-being

Chakras

Chakras is the name for our body's energy centres, like the heart, the navel, and the mind. These are closely related to the areas of excretion glands and the endocrine system, like the adrenals, the thymus, and the pineal gland. Sexual trauma affects all our chakras but specifically four of the energy systems in our bodies.

The first one is obviously the *root chakra*. This is connected to our sense of safety, security, and basic human needs, such as connecting with others and our Mother Earth. When it's traumatized, we lose those important feelings of being safe and protected, especially if the trauma was inflicted by a family member. We lose the sense of being safe and comfortable at home. We can't trust anyone, because we're not sure who to trust.

When this chakra, which is located between your sexual organs and anus, becomes traumatized through forced or coerced sex, you consciously block the area to avoid having to remember what happened. It can cause sexual dysfunction and relationship issues.

The trauma eventually gets pushed into Pandora's box, and you move on with your life, but you continue having issues experiencing pleasures in life. Which brings us to the second chakra that's affected: the *sacral chakra*, the energy centre from which we experience the butterflies and the pleasures of life in general. It is also the seat of our power together with the solar plexus.

This relates to personal power that's also affected by sexual trauma. The trauma takes away your ability to be confident, and you'll feel shameful about yourself, with or without the conscious memory of what happened to you. This is because, energetically speaking, the trauma sits inside your body until you consciously take care of it and heal it. It's stored in your body, and this is known as *cell memory* or *body memory*. It will affect you even though you can't remember it anymore. You can tell not just by how you respond to life but also if you tune in to this part of your body and perhaps notice a strange pull, a lump, or a worrying sensation. It's a clue to what you need to work on and heal.

Another chakra that's affected is the *heart chakra*, which is related to feeling compassionate and loving toward yourself and others. It's the chakra that helps us connect with others in a meaningful way. During trauma, this chakra shuts down to protect us from feeling the emotional pain resulting from the trauma. We realize that the people we rely on, trust, and love don't have our best interest in mind, and we need to protect ourselves from this realization.

The heart chakra reacts when we experience emotional trauma, which often goes hand in hand with sexual trauma perpetrated by a parent. We may be unable to make meaningful connections or find that we only feel compassionate or sympathetic toward people we aren't related to. We may even feel that we only connect to animals, stuffed animals, or other things. As a child, I connected deeply to my stuffed animals, gifts I received, and even clothing I wore, more so than I did to my parents. This may seem odd, but it's understandable considering my traumas.

As a child and later as an adult, I found myself emotionally attaching to others and things in an unhealthy way, constantly looking for that emotional fulfillment from outside myself. It caused even more pain and suffering when that emotional need was repeatedly unfulfilled in the way I was hoping for. Again, this shows the importance of coming home to the self.

The next chakra that's important to mention is the *throat chakra*. After the #MeToo movement and with recent issues that emerged in the government of the United States about sexual abuse claims made against people in high places, the reactions from the public were rather disturbing. So many claimed that the allegations weren't true or that they didn't believe the victim. The percentage of false claims is extremely low, maybe between 1 and 3 percent.

The reality is that people who don't want to believe it will not believe it no matter what you say. This can have detrimental consequences for the victim. As children, we're not believed and even gaslighted. As adults, remembering the abuse twenty or even fifty years later, we're once again not being believed. It's difficult to believe yourself after being called a liar as a child and shutting down memory recall when you were a teen because of shaming.

I remember feeling so deeply embarrassed over it that I literally felt faint, and seconds later I couldn't recall what I had just been thinking about. It's important to let a victim talk about it. The throat chakra is the one that's affected most during and after assaults. We're told not to speak, that someone will hurt our pet, our stuffy, our sister, our mother, or who knows what if we say anything to anyone ever. We may even have experienced an attempt to murder us. This takes our voices away.

Basically, sexual abuse removes our sense of safety, belonging, and confidence. It makes us feel deeply and gravely ashamed over something that wasn't even our fault. It stops us from being able to make deep, meaningful connections to others. This often leads to many failed relationships and to us not being able to express ourselves. We fail with work, art, writing, talking; we faint in a speech or lose our train of thought. We may experience difficulties getting a job or a career.

Life becomes beyond difficult and feels like a drag. Everything just becomes too hard to deal with, and we're unable to make decisions or use the power of our voice to create the life we really deserve. We simply cannot speak.

It saddens me deeply every time I think about this. Our silent suffering goes completely unnoticed by others. Here's a poem I once wrote to somehow explain what it feels like:

> I am sorry if I couldn't speak up about the abuse when I should have,
>> because I couldn't make sense of it
>> and because my power to speak was taken.
> I am sorry you cannot believe me now
>> because it has been over twenty years since the abuse stopped.
> I am sorry you cannot emphasize with me
>> and you choose the side of my abusers
>> because you feel it is too horrible to be true.
> But in fact, it happened, and I am sorry,
>> but I will speak and never stop.
> I will not apologize for speaking up.
>> I will not apologize for finally connecting with my true self.
>> I will not apologize for being able to understand the things that were done.

Because it is important today for me and all of you
>to know that by understanding what happened,
>you can finally understand why you were the way you were.

And everything will finally make sense.
>Life is no longer confusing to us.
>This frees us. This realigns our chakras and heals them.

Speaking up shows that I am healing.
>Telling me not to write or not to speak only shows that you
>lack the ability to understand or have compassion for others.

I stopped apologizing for who I was
>the minute I understood myself and took back my power.

Finally, there's the *third eye chakra* and the *crown chakra*. The top chakras are related to vision, hearing, sensing, memory, connection to your higher self, orientation, and balance. I suffered from vertigo my whole life and lacked the ability to remember things. I'd lose my train of thought so often people would think I was stupid or that there was something wrong with me. I lost my ability to study and focus on work. I turned anger into depression and suffered from anxiety that I couldn't explain. A functioning third eye is crucial to envision and have clarity and direction in life.

The trauma also suppressed my spiritual gifts. I couldn't understand guidance from my higher self because energetically, I was blocking it. The pineal gland sits very close to the part of the brain that stores memories connected to emotion, and somehow it was affecting my ability to have visions, as I was blocking off the experiences.

I was also blocking my gifts of clairvoyance, clairaudience, and claircognizance. For some reason, it didn't affect the other *clairs* as much, but the ones connected to the eyes, ears, and brain were certainly influenced. It took me between two and three years of eating clean, adding antioxidants and supplements like ginkgo biloba, and eating a diet rich in pineal gland detoxifying substances to recover this. As a small child, I had fantastic visions and clear auditory skills. I lost it all due to trauma. I'm still working on recovering it and retraining my psychic muscles. If I can do that, I know it's possible for you as well.

Being able to communicate with spirit in an effortless, flowing way is your God-given right. Realigning your energy centres and healing yourself allows you to function the way you're supposed to. This reinstates your power and lets you integrate your inspiration into this world in ways that are unique to you. After all, you're a creative being, a multidimensional true co-creator and child of God, my loves.

To retrieve memories and to understand your physical traumas, you need to re-establish your relationship with your body by listening to its whispers. Feel into it and learn how to describe your sensations in relation to certain thoughts and triggers. To understand what's happening in your body and mind, sit with yourself and ask yourself about what certain physical feelings mean.

If you feel a lump in your throat or a squeezing in your heart, for example, sit with it and ask where it's from and what originally caused it, then write down your impressions and insights in your journal. Your body has stored all your trauma, so to uncover it, you need to be willing to connect to it. I've included instructions below on how you can realign your energy centres to rebalance yourself.

Reconnecting Mind to Heart

You may wonder what this means and why it's so important. Many people in this world have experienced some sort of trauma. Some undoubtedly have been worse than others, but what it does is sever the connection between your mind and your heart or also between your mind and your body. As the body experiences trauma and the heart feels heavy and pain-stricken from the emotions that come forward, your mind will try to protect you by disconnecting from the harsh realities of your life and the world.

This especially happens if you were a child at the time, to protect you. Your mind can't make sense of it, and the realities are too harsh to be accepted by the young mind. You become disconnected from your heart, body, and ability to remember. Dissociation ensues, with an inability to be inside your body. This also may give you an inability to feel compassion for others, especially your own family, if a family member was the cause of your pain.

You may find that you connect better with strangers or feel deeply compassionate for people you hear about on the news but have little compassion or even sympathy for other adults in your family. You may even say that you only have a heart for animals, not humans. You disconnect from people who might cause you pain. You disconnect selectively from your heart. You also disconnect from your body, so you don't have to deal with the body's memories.

You're not heartless. You have a deeply compassionate heart but have sheltered it out of fear. When you reconnect heart and mind, all the memories and sensations will come back. This might happen suddenly or occur slowly over time. Often, it's triggered by an intense emotional trauma in your adult life.

Reconnecting your heart and mind is essential to being able to understand yourself. It's also essential to be able to feel compassion for yourself. When you get to this point, you're healing from your trauma. Compassion is love. Compassion turns to forgiveness, for yourself and for others. It may seem like a long haul, but trust yourself to get there one day. You can reconnect gently through meditation and the previously mentioned methods to connect with your true self—your authentic, real, true self.

I took an amazing course a few years ago that helped me to energetically reconnect with myself, including my body, heart, mind, and spirit. Let yourself be guided by your spirit and take inspired action along your healing path, which will guide you to wherever you need to go.

The severance between heart and mind can be envisioned in a particular way. There's an energy body that circles through the heart. There's a small one around the tiny space known as the zero-gravity point of the heart and a large one around our whole body, as well as an energy body that circles our brain. The one around our brain often circles much faster, as these days many people are fairly mind-centred, which hangs together with the education system, electronics, distractions, and a disinterest in connecting with one's body and Mother Earth. If the head spins faster than the body, you basically decapitate yourself, and the connection between heart and mind is broken. Refocusing and paying attention to how you feel inside your body and heart can help realign this system.

This requires you to practice moving your spirit out of your brain and down into the rest of what makes you into you. This is where meditation can help you to recalibrate yourself. Meditation is a way to slow down the mind's spinning cycle so it gets a chance to recalibrate and reconnect to the heart, where the true reason for your existence resides. The heart carries the wisdom of your true purpose here on Earth, your reason for existing, your *why*.

Slowing down the mind helps you on your path to reconnect to your *why*, your passion, and your purpose in life. It will also help you to tune in with your body in order to recover body memories and recall your truth. In meditation, we use our breath and dive into our body to reconnect with ourselves.

Please understand the importance of slowing down and reconnecting with your body and your heart. The expression "running around like a chicken without a head" describes exactly what it feels like when you're disconnected from your heart and your life's purpose. You're all over the place, distracted easily, and running around with an agenda, forgetting the reason for doing it. This leads to chaos.

Stop yourself, settle down, and reconnect every day. Make it a vital priority and a normal way to start your day. Do yourself this favour.

Methods that assist in awakening and healing yourself include the following:

- energy healing to fix leaks in aura
- reiki as a self-healing tool
- meditation to connect with your soul
- qigong for energy maintenance
- essential oils and whole-food supplements to assist the natural healing abilities of your body and mind
- Awakening the Illuminated Heart workshop (ATIH) to reconnect your heart and mind and open your awareness
- going within regularly to check in with yourself and how you feel
- journaling your thoughts and experiences and memories to remember and be clear-minded
- expressing your emotions for self-acknowledgment
- creating from the heart for joy and to feel worthy
- spending time in nature to reconnect with your Earth mother
- connecting authentically with others through the heart to feel compassion and connection with the world
- speaking your mind to voice your true thoughts and create boundaries and to help yourself and others to understand

The Effect on Your Family

I just wanted to mention that you're not the only one who suffers from the issues that were loaded onto you as a child. Your family suffers, your spouse suffers, and other people you meet before you know what happened to you suffer. Therefore, it's important for you to remember what happened to you and to be able to heal.

Healing is possible, and it's your right to heal yourself. It's not your fault that this happened. However, as an adult, you have a responsibility to find yourself again and to heal all of you. You can then go on and start rebuilding your life on a solid foundation. If you're building a life but not taking care of your shadow self, you're on shaky ground.

Trust me here. You may be able to build something great. but it will all come tumbling down the day your other self decides to come out and cause a disturbance. You can't, and shouldn't, keep stuffing down your abuser's dirty laundry. It's time to air out the dirty laundry, take a closer look at the stains, and figure out their origins.

You may be confronted with resistance from family members and friends, but remember how much you've given to others in your life. Now that it's your turn to give to yourself, others will have to learn to accept that and give you the space for it to happen. If they don't, you'll have no choice but to take the space and time for yourself.

It's hard for others to see their family change into something they no longer recognize, but we all change. The only constant is change, is what I like to tell people. We're always transforming, transfiguring and trans-mutating ourselves and our lives. It's a natural process of growth and being an adult of multidimensionality. Nothing ever stays the same, and hopefully you have people in your life who can understand that and are supportive. If not, do what's right for you.

Forgiveness

Finally, we come to forgiveness. It's a word that's often thrown around by people who feel you should just get over what happened in your past. Well, some may actually understand this, but many who tell you to try to forgive simply don't understand what it's like to be severely abused for years and then wake up a couple of decades later to the realization of the extent of the abuse, having to relive everything. This is followed by years of therapy, working to get to the point where we finally feel well enough to talk about it and express the unspeakable. And now, suddenly, we're asked to forgive and move on?

Forgiveness is your choice. You're not required to forgive and forget. If you choose to forgive, do it for yourself. Forgive yourself for not being adult enough to handle the atrocities, for not being able to understand what happened, for not being able to speak up about it for forty years, and for not being able to remember the exact details of what happened. When you forgive yourself and show yourself the compassion you truly deserve, you'll find yourself in a place from which you can forgive the world for just being the world. It is as it is, and you'll see that one day, when you're ready. You'll find a way of forgiveness that certainly doesn't require you to keep in contact with abusive people.

You can forgive but don't forget, ever again, as this has now become your power. Your power is reinstated, and you can speak, move, and act with confidence, becoming the confident self you were always meant to be. You've also grown exponentially, so don't let anyone take that power away from you again. It's yours, so do something creative with it.

I forgave the moment I started to look at my life as a story. Everything that happened has now become just a part of my story. I laugh over some parts, cry over others, but essentially, it's my story, and I own that. Take back your power, survivor, and own that story. It is *your* truth.

I found that the path of forgiveness reappears in our lives in different settings. You may have to forgive many people—not just the abusers of your past but ex-spouses and friends. I found when I began to surrender to the present and accept how things are that a miracle would happen, and my stressed relationships with others suddenly became bearable and even began moving in a better direction that worked for everyone. Things aren't always as bad as they may look at first glance.

I discovered that reiki created for me a life of healing on multiple levels. Its power is sensed and felt through all of the relationships in my life, and my ability to master life and death has become a constant state of being, easily navigated through infinite intent. I wish that for all of you.

Ultimate forgiveness relates directly to the amount of self-love and self-compassion you carry and have achieved on your healing journey. In a pure state of love, joy, and bliss, you'll have released all the blame, guilt, and shame you harboured in yourself. This automatically extends into your field and allows for the ultimate forgiveness, which is equal to ultimate freedom. Forgiveness simply happens when we embrace all our emotions and are at peace with them.

CHAPTER 9
Empath Versus Narcissist

W HY AM I INCLUDING THIS subject here, and why combine the spiritual and the psychological? Well, there's little to no difference. As all our bodies are one, the psychological is just another expression of the spiritual. With holistic healing, we consider the whole of ourselves and only separate to understand what's happening.

Separation is an illusion we create to gain perception. You can apply that to pretty much any situation. Any disorder that's currently being diagnosed is simply the diagnosis of an array of symptoms and disease presentation. They give it a name to explain what's happening. They create a separation to explain it or describe the issue so they can treat it.

When we separate things out, we create space and time, seeing the illness as a separate entity when it's not. The symptoms you exhibit are due to an underlying original problem. There may be a few things that led up to this issue. Any illness originated from an imbalance, but it may take some detective work to figure out what truly caused the imbalance.

I found some amazing insights in one of Louise Hay's books, *You Can Heal Your Life*, which details illnesses and the underlying imbalance that leads to the manifestation. If you're in denial or shying away from certain ideas, you won't figure it out. You'll simply accept a doctor's decision and label for your "mental illness" and take that pill to numb it out.

Eventually we may figure out that we'd been avoiding issues that led up to behaviours and exposures to something that spiralled into the expression of an illness. Often, we never figure out the true cause. It may be physical, emotional, or psychological in nature. Sometimes we're predisposed to a condition due to genetics, environment, or family settings.

Being predisposed doesn't always mean that you'll be affected. That's why it's important to become aware of yourself and your surroundings, the situations you live in or grew up with, and how they've affected and programmed your behaviour. You have innate healing powers that, once activated, can heal pretty much anything. You won't learn that in school, and no doctor will tell you about it, because it's not taught in medical schools.

This is something that activates when you go within and retreat. Ancient cultures knew about this. Shamans know about this, and spiritual healers generally are aware of it as well. In fact, we can produce our own antioxidants: a cancer-fighting, brain-structure-recovering, inflammatory-processes-reversing superpower. I believe anyone is capable of doing this, but not everyone will do so in this lifetime.

Empaths

We've used the word *empath* to label someone who exhibits an array of symptoms that explain their experiences and who they are. It's a broad term and has been misunderstood and judged many times over. *Empath* describes a being that is sensitive to another's emotions and its surroundings. In my opinion, empaths are simply psychics, a new word for an old paradigm. Many people have misconceptions about psychics, and so this new term has developed.

Most newly realized empaths are immature and struggle with issues that stem from their ability to assimilate with other beings. They're incredibly open and haven't learned how to manage their energy. Many are leaking the energy out, mainly due to a lack of understanding about who they are, but also often due to abusive situations in which they've found themselves, often since childhood. Sexual abuse specifically creates a leak of energy in the root chakra, which means they have very little ability to protect themselves from people who'll take advantage of their good nature. It's a weakness that needs to be corrected.

We create our own realities. You can decide to be closed to energy, or you can decide to be open to it. That's the power your mind has. The only limit is the one your mind created for you. In truth, we're multidimensional beings and always have been, but programming of our minds has kept many in an unconscious or unawakened state of being.

In 2017, I went to a shaman to talk about this spirit that has been following me since I was a child. My intention was to find out how to remove it. On the day I wanted to make the appointment, I broke my leg. When I eventually called to make the appointment, the shaman laughed and said that it happens often. Many of her clients had to reschedule because something abrupt happened on the day of the spirit removal.

The belief of entity or attachment is in fact commonly reported by empaths. There's always a story behind it, but generally, I feel it's more related to the energy you give to this entity, spirit, belief, or idea. In fact, after it's removed, you'll often start to realize a truth about yourself, over which you may have been in denial. Many times, entities are a part of a body memory, masking it, and the spirit distracts from the truth of what lies behind this memory.

In addition, when we leak out energy, spirits, animals, and people tend to be highly attracted to us and latch on. It creates an unhealthy synergy or relationship based on our good nature giving our energy away freely. This often leaves us drained, exhausted, depressed, or experiencing ups and downs.

So-called demonic or energy attachments are created by simply not being in your full power and letting fear and worries control your actions and beliefs. It's a real and true experience, but when you begin to grow into higher dimensional levels of consciousness, you'll find all those low-energy experiences beginning to disappear as you become empowered and nearly invisible to it. You basically disappear from that lower energetic vibration. It can no longer attach because you're at a much higher stage of vibration and are living at a different dimensional level.

It's sort of like a game that kids play where players pretend the floor is lava and they must avoid touching the surface, as it would kill them. The players stay off the floor by standing on furniture. Staying on higher ground prevents them from getting burned, but that doesn't mean you can just stop doing energy maintenance. You can't just stop taking a shower to stay clean. It all goes hand in hand: one washes the other. As you grow accustomed to your spiritual practices, everything begins to flow with ease.

So, what exactly is energy? Energy is the effect of how we feel, as emotion and energy are woven together. E-motion means energy in motion, and as I explained before, it's closely connected to organs that produce hormones, like the pituitary gland, the adrenals, the pineal, and others.

Regular energy maintenance can help you create a clear energy field by regulating your emotions, especially if you also work with spirit regularly. You'll find it important to create a regular energy-clearing practice, which I recommend that everyone should do. Just because you aren't open to it doesn't mean it can't influence you. Energy clearing can help dissolve disruptive and intrusive thoughts and can help you feel more safe and secure in your home and in your body. It truly is an amazing tool. As a sensitive person, you'll always be open to those experiences, and so energy-clearing is vital.

It's also important to learn how to keep your energy bank full and have any leaks plugged, your chakras aligned, and your light body activated and running smoothly. Not having a full energy bank often extends into the physical and leaves your bank account dry as well. If you struggle with finances, this may be a sign that you need to do some work on yourself.

You can ask a reputable shaman for help with plugging leaks or attend a mediumship course or a reiki attunement to begin to learn more about energy and how to maintain yours. I've added a chakra-balancing technique that will also help fix imbalances.

The more you work on yourself, the less you'll feel like a victim of circumstance. This may initially be about protecting, but it's much more about empowering and strengthening yourself, which is essentially much more effective than protection methods. Yet in the beginning, it's important to practice what makes you feel safe in your home and in your body to emerge from the fear state. Allow yourself to grow from an immature empath into an adept and eventually a master empath.

Narcissists

If you're an empath who's experienced the synergy between you and a narcissist, your energy may be especially weakened. The more and the longer you expose yourself to that, the weaker you'll get, as the narcissist who suffers from severe low self-esteem will latch onto you to empower himself. This energy exchange isn't an exchange at all but more like vampirism. It will eventually suck you dry, and that's when the narcissist will likely have found a new victim. He'll only move on if he found another victim.

Narcissists don't generate their own energy but rather suck others dry to feed their ego. For example, a narcissist will make jokes about you behind your back or right in front of you. He'll take what you say and turn it against you. He'll try to make you doubt yourself, bringing up things from the past, blaming you for mishaps, questioning your sanity or ability to take care of your house or children, or claiming your job is easy in order to make you look stupid. Then he turns around and compliments or love bombs you to keep you emotionally trapped.

Sadly, we often become very insecure and begin to worry that we may lose our children in a divorce or not receive any child support. A separation can be exceedingly difficult in this type of relationship because of the narcissist's tendency to triangulate his victims. Narcissists will make you look like a horrible person behind your back to your friends, family, and even your co-workers. They may call your therapist and ask about your mental health or try to convince your friends to spill the beans about your issues. They'll then use that as collateral against you in court or during separation proceedings. It's all an effort to destroy your social support so that they can have the upper hand. It may not be something you'd ever consider doing to someone, and it may be a bit of a shock to find out what's happening.

In the field of the one, we acknowledge and celebrate differences. We see the beauty this synergy of energies has brought to help us understand ourselves. The narcissist becomes the gift we received to help us see ourselves more clearly and recognize what needs to be healed and loved within us. When we get to the place where we recognize that the experience with a narcissist actually triggered and catapulted us into an awakening and expanded our horizons and our growth, we can even forgive the narcissist for his part in our story.

Don't think psychics aren't able to be narcissistic. I encountered psychics in my childhood who had narcissistic tendencies. They were usually the type who didn't work heart-centred, meaning they were only interested in being right and didn't care about the effect their words had on their clients. Such psychics may be trying to intentionally steal your energy, as they're unable to retain their own. Those people aren't healers. They are pretenders, so be careful who you trust.

CHAPTER 10

Taking Care of Yourself

YOUR HEALTH IS AT THE forefront. You need to be at your peak to be able to handle all the work and stress that accompanies recovering memories and dealing with family and interpersonal issues. Many people decide to take a year off to figure this out. Most of us can't afford to be off for that long, but you also can't afford not to work through these things. What you can do is reduce toxins in your environment, including toxic thoughts and people.

Remove yourself from situations where you feel anxious, but try not to alienate yourself completely. It's okay to take time away from people. You're going through a lot and need to sort this out with yourself. Other people may try to influence you or even manipulate your thinking. Consult a great trauma specialist. You deserve it and need the best you can get. Friends may not always be the best choice to trust with such sensitive information, so choose wisely.

Work on establishing a healthy environment so your brain has all the nutrients and supplies it needs to function at its peak. Exercise your brain and mental capacities. Journal your every thought and emotion. Figure yourself out. Eat a healthy diet that supports brain health. Use essential oils that support a healthy brain and decrease anxiety. Look into adrenal health, research it, and follow what you're being guided to do.

Practice your intuition, which is your internal guidance system. It may not work properly due to the abuse, as you were repeatedly told that you were wrong about your intuitive insights, making you lose your ability to trust your own guidance system. We call this *being counterintuitive*. As you change your trauma brain with all the work you do on yourself, your intuitive guidance also will be recovering. You'll finally be able to understand it and make the right decisions for yourself.

You went through something incredible. Your story is unique, and you need to realize that you're lucky to be alive today. Be thankful for every breath and the possibility to create a beautiful life from now on. Beyond recovery is the start of a beautiful life for you and the family that's still with you. Whatever happened in your past doesn't define you, but it does make you wiser and stronger. It gives you the ability to live a more purposeful and inspiring life. Do everything you always wanted to do that you felt you couldn't because of all the negative thoughts toward yourself.

You can do anything you want; the possibilities are endless. You're a creation of God and have the power to co-create with god. That's your birthright. Your father in heaven and your mother on Earth want you to be empowered, just like any loving and encouraging parent would want you to do.

Some people feel that it's not possible to reintegrate or get the soul pieces back together and into your body. However, I know that it's possible, and once you've done it, you'll solidly stand in your power and be able to express yourself without losing your train of thought in front of a group of people. You'll be fully able to talk about what you endured as a child. When you reintegrate, you can not only make sense of your experiences but also talk about them and express them without dissociating. You can write and teach about your own story, like the confident and happy self you were always meant to be.

I'm doing it right now. Others have done it too, and so can you. It just takes time and inner self-work. Everyone's on their own journey at their own pace. Don't judge yourself by how fast or how much you can remember or how far you've progressed in a certain time frame. Some of us may not remember everything, and that's completely okay. You'll only remember as much as your mind allows you to know, as much as you can possibly process.

Trust in yourself and the process of unfoldment, which you are undergoing. Show yourself all the love and nurturing you deserve. As a survivor, you deserve it as much as anyone, if not more. Please put yourself first, dear one. You can't give to others from an empty cup, and yours was empty for an exceedingly long time. It's now time to fill up your own cup, have your own back, and love and nurture your inner child the way it was supposed to happen. Today, you can take responsibility for the child you once were. Today, you can take back your power and fully and graciously stand within it.

I hope I can reach many people like myself with this and that I can inspire others to live their true authentic lives, taking back the power that was taken from them. The truth is hard to swallow, but I want you to have the courage to know and see it as it really is. This is a journey of self-discovery. This is how we can transform our world into a place where we all can prosper and work together on the project called humanity. In unity, peace, love, and light, we can uncover the darkness and shine our bright lights straight at it. No more hiding. This is finally your moment to come out of the survivor closet and move into the thriving seat.

Self-Care Techniques

I started using an energy-clearing and grounding salt scrub after I began working with spirit, during the time when I still felt heavily affected by my past. The point is to remove the heavy energies that surrounds you so that your mind can be clear and your emotions can be understood. When you understand yourself, it's much easier to cope with life. It's also great for your skin and mood in general. It made a tremendous difference for me from an energetic point of view, so I feel compelled to include this information here.

Keep the scrub in a container and use it every time you shower. Gently scrub it over you from top to bottom. Avoid sensitive areas, as the salt will burn open wounds, eyes, and other intimate areas and may be harsh for some bathtubs. Always rinse with plenty of water afterward. Here's the recipe.

- 1 cup fine sea salt and/or Himalayan salt
- 60 ml (4 tbsp) olive oil or fractionated coconut oil
- 5 drops frankincense essential oil
- 5 drops clary sage essential oil
- 5 drops patchouli essential oil
- 4 drops tea tree essential oil, used as a preservative

You can use all four oils or just one or two. Simply add a few more drops if using only one or two oils. You can also choose oils that you prefer that are grounding and protective or uplifting. Make sure to keep a few drops of frankincense in it, though, since that's the main and most important part of this specific scrub.

Mix it all up clockwise with a spoon while saying a prayer to call upon the archangels Michael and Raphael or any others you choose, in order to infuse their energies and the intention for the user of the scrub to be protected. You may also add healing reiki energy to the mixture.

Always use pure, unadulterated, and safe oils for your products. Do your research, as you don't want oils that could cause skin issues or contain anything that you don't want in your brain. That defeats the purpose. We're aiming to remove toxins from your body and mind, not add new ones.

Realigning Your Energy Centres

Chakras can be opened and aligned using frequencies like sound and vibration, essential oils, visualizations, colours, and a healthy diet. As chakras align with the body's energy systems and hormonal glands, diet can be an important factor in your health and your chakras' health. They go hand in hand; these aren't separate things at all. Understand that your spiritual, mental, emotional, and physical bodies are the same and not separate from one another. This means that you need to treat your body like the sacred temple it is.

There are certain vibrational sounds that can be used to align your chakras and clear out what doesn't belong. These also assist in awakening and may ease you into higher levels of consciousness if practiced regularly. During the time I went through the recalling of memories, I tried to do this without the knowledge of the sounds that were related to the chakras and became frustrated that I lacked this wisdom. It's important to know how you can align yourself, and it may assist you during moments of anxiety. It may trigger a kundalini awakening.

If you find energy changes in your body or vibrations or jerking of muscles at some point, don't be alarmed, as this is normal and part of the body's rewiring process during awakenings. I've experienced many of these, and each time I experienced an increase in awareness afterward. I have found this method to be very energizing and relaxing to the body and mind. I was taught this by a friend and meditation facilitator. I wish I'd have practiced this more often and sooner, so I wanted to make sure to include this invaluable method here for you.

Before starting this, ground yourself by imagining roots growing out of your feet deeply into the ground. It helps to feel grounded and settled while you work on your chakras. The following are the sounds for each chakra:

- *LAM*—root chakra, red/magenta
- *VAM*—sacral chakra, orange
- *RAM*—solar chakra, golden yellow
- *YAM*—heart chakra, emerald green or pink
- *HAM*—throat chakra, lapis blue

- *OM*—third-eye chakra, indigo or violet. You can also use *SHAM* or *FEW*.
- *AAH*—crown chakra, pearlescent white or violet. You can also use *OM* instead, since this frequency can open the crown.

With each sound, observe the chakra in your mind or feel into it. Notice how the vibration is felt inside your body. You may see colours and light or just feel the effect. If you feel or see nothing, don't worry. There's no goal except to express the sounds repeatedly, one by one. You don't have to see or feel it to experience the effect. The more aware you become of yourself, the more you'll be able to witness what's happening.

Merkabah Light Explosion

This is the best and simplest way to protect yourself and to clear energies in your field and surroundings. It's also a more advanced method that may not be for everybody, so use what works best for you. I knew about this for a long time but found it was also taught in reiki attunements and in Drunvalo Melchizedek's teachings.

A *Merkabah* describes the light body and means "light-spirit-body." It's the light vessel that carries your spirit and your body. There are techniques to activate it that are taught by different teachers all over the world, but I'll only share with you my own quite simple technique. This helps you feel safe and protected, empowers your being, and works to bring balance back into your life.

Before you begin, take a few deep breaths, or do some qigong movements or something else that brings awareness back to yourself. Connect to Mother Earth by growing roots to her centre and send her your love, then open to Father Sky and let his light enter you. Let the seed of his light merge with your heart as Mother Earth's love rises and enters your heart as well.

Begin to see or feel the swirling of green and pink colours that turn into white sparkling light. Become aware of your energy field, then see or feel the light grow slowly, intensifying in light and brightness, until it feels like it's going to explode within you. Take a deep breath and let the ball of light explode inside your body on your outbreath. See the light extending to your sides like wings, rapidly engulfing your very being and extending as far out as you can make it go.

As it explodes, say the word *Merkabah*. See the light moving through the walls, furniture, pets, family, your town, the city, or even the continent. Observe or know that your light body is moving at perfect speed, clearing and cleansing all in its path, then let it reach equilibrium and bask in the energy. You can envision yourself in it or feel the tingle all over your body, just knowing that it's working.

In the beginning, you may not feel or see much, but know that your pure intention is doing it. It's working, and until you're more aware, you may not actually see it or feel it. Your awareness still has some growing to do, that's all.

I use this all the time, and it completely activates me and clears out all negative lower vibrational energies in an instant. Using your breath during this meditation is essential, as well as when you do other energy-clearing techniques like qigong or reiki. Breath is your life force energy. It increases your levels of awareness and shifts your consciousness.

Inner Child Connection

In fall of 2016, after I'd recalled the birth of my daughter, which I had also repressed, I was going within and trying to reconnect to parts of me from which I felt disconnected. I had an exceedingly difficult time bringing up my emotions about the events. I needed to sit with myself and dig deep for the feelings I'd buried for more than twenty years. I was going into a meditative state, in which I pulled up the image of my younger self. It was a memory of a time after I'd been raped. I found myself in the bathroom, behind a locked door, looking at myself in the mirror.

I looked distraught. My hair was messy, and I was wearing glasses. My eyes looked unfocused, and I tried to connect with the person in the mirror to see how she was feeling. I was playing out the memory as I remembered it, almost as if I was watching a movie inside my mind. My younger self, about 12 years old, was in shock and crying but afraid of my abuser hearing. He was sitting in the living room, reading a newspaper.

I was staring at myself in the mirror. *What had just happened?* I'd woken up cold and shivering. I quickly went to the bathroom and cleaned myself up. I brushed my hair, but the brush was getting stuck. My hair was messy, and I felt angry at myself. I was angry at the brush, angry at my hair, angry at my image in the mirror, angry at the world, and angry at myself for being just a stupid kid who didn't understand anything.

I was also angry at myself for being clumsy, and I was even angry at myself for being angry. I wanted to throw the brush, but he would have heard that, so I bit myself on my arm with all the strength I could muster, until I left deep purple marks on my skin. It hurt but not nearly as much as the gaping hole in my heart. It did not hurt as much as … *what just happened?*

A flashback appeared as I looked at my face in the mirror, my steel-blue eyes staring angrily back at me. No, I didn't want to go there. But I had to.

I am here with you, so allow yourself to know. I know it's hard, but you can do it.

My adult voice travelled through time, reaching the mind of my younger self. She was surprised and saw her face softening in the mirror.

The one you should direct your anger toward isn't you but the man sitting in the living room, reading the paper. He did this to you, and you know it.

My younger self turned her head in the direction where he was sitting, then nodded slowly. Realization crossed over her face. Her feelings changed from anger to despair. Her forehead wrinkled, and she opened her mouth. She could barely bring out the words, almost a whispering.

"I got raped …"

She quickly she put her hand back over her mouth, as if trying to stop herself from speaking the unspeakable.

Repressed crying into her hand, tears falling from her long eyelashes, she heard a voice in the distance ask if everything was okay in the bathroom. I reconnected and spoke to her.

I'm here, and I can hear you. I know how you feel, and I'll always be there for you.

"Who are you? Are you God?" my younger self asked.

I am you, and you are me.

My younger self looked confused, wondering how this was possible.

"Are you my older self?"

There was no answer. We were also going to get interrupted, as the abuser knocked on the door.

"I'll be out in a minute!" she said.

My younger self was cleaning her tears with a tissue and washing her hands, collecting her thoughts. She then turned to the side.

"Whoever you are, please take me with you. I don't want to stay here anymore. Save me."

But I couldn't do that. I could only be there with her in her thoughts through our connection.

At the time this happened, I didn't know that what I'd done was called *inner child work*. I can remember me at that age talking to my older self. Here's my explanation of how this works: Time isn't linear. Its linearity is an illusion of the human mind, a faulty belief that's ingrained into us since childhood. Time is circular, like a spiral. We remove the separation linearity creates and blend our experiences together, which then allows us to travel in time.

It can happen through our emotions, bringing up a feeling and connecting it to a memory. With our intention, we create a bridge in time, which allows us to connect and support ourselves on our journey. Some of us can even create this bridge to other people and places through time and not only to ourselves. You see, the connection between our memories and emotions needs to work. If it's broken, we become handicapped and vulnerable.

Time Travel Exercise

The only requirement for this exercise is to leave all your fears, ego, and beliefs at the door before you enter. You may not enter with a fearful heart. Most of us at this point are likely to have already left behind many fears. Please note that if you're fearful of this exercise, don't do it. Instead, work more on building your trust in yourself.

The first part is a grounding exercise, and I recommend that anyone should do this, as it will help you become more grounded and stable. It helps release some of the stagnant energies in your mind from the recalling of memories. Your head may be terribly busy, and I encourage you to engage in grounding exercises regularly.

Find a comfortable place where you won't be disturbed. Drink a cup of water before you start, and use any essential oils you'd like to include during your meditation. A sitting position is best, as it prevents you from falling asleep.

Take a few deep and slow breaths, filling your lungs and body with life force energy. You can imagine it as drawing in white light and expelling grey matter when you breathe out.

Connect to Mother Earth by imagining growing roots out of the centre of your belly, through your root chakra, and all the way out to her centre, where you wrap your roots around the core to anchor yourself. Feel the sensation of being anchored by swaying gently from left to right, feeling this deep connectedness as if you're a human pendulum.

See your heart illuminated in pink and send some of that light down alongside your roots to her core, feeling the love and compassion in your heart for her. When it reaches her core, see it light up and rejoice delightfully. Notice a green light emerging from her core, traveling up your roots until it enters your body, all the way to your heart, where it combines with your pink light. This is her response to your loving connection. Mother Earth is letting you know that she loves you too.

The light from your heart travels up to the top of your head, where it emerges in the form of a beautiful pink lotus flower. As your crown chakra opens, somewhere out in space, a star lights up as it notices you, and the light travels down to touch the top of your head. The bright light of Father Sky enters your being and travels to your heart, where it merges with the green and the pink light.

The energy ball grows inside your heart until it explodes into a bright starburst, engulfing your whole being and beyond. Allow yourself to rest in the glory of white sacred light, feeling yourself become weightless in its soothing, healing presence. It's all you. You're a divine being of this universe. Ask your angels and guides to help you on your journey into your past.

Now, feel your body. Can you feel any emotional parts? Ask to be reconnected with the original cause of this emotional pain inside your body—then, with intention, travel along the emotional cord into your past. Pull up an image from your past, a memory, where you'd felt this exact same way. Don't worry if you can't access an image immediately or if you aren't sure if it's the right one. Anything that happens will be the right thing for you at this moment in time. Trust your higher self.

When you have your memory, an image, or a sequence, look at yourself and feel into the moment. What did it feel like? What were your thoughts? What were you doing? What just happened? Go through the memory and don't worry if you can't remember some segments; it will all come back one day if it must.

Try to connect with your younger self through your thoughts. Ask if your younger self can hear you and watch the reaction. Notice in yourself if you remember hearing a voice in that moment when you were a child. Can you recall hearing the voice of your older self? If you find this connection, and your younger self needs comfort, give it. Send loving messages of support, but never lie or pretend about anything.

Tell your younger self that you can see everything and that their emotions are valid. Tell them that you understand what they are going through, that you know, that you'll be there to support them during their life and always have their back. Mention the things you'd have wanted to hear as a child, but never promise anything you know can't happen.

You may send messages of hope, for example. If you have a great marriage or children, tell them about that because if they need to hear that, and you'll know that, this will give them hope, and they'll feel comfort, love, and compassion from you. If you have nothing positive to share, just provide your comfort and support.

Don't stay in the past for too long. Once you've done what you intended to do, say your goodbyes and gently move back into the present moment. Don't be afraid of getting lost during this, because you didn't go anywhere. You simply accessed the past from your present moment and within your own sovereign being. You were at home all along. Trust yourself.

After you return from this meditative state, remember to take a few deep breaths and a few sips of water. Don't move, but just stay relaxed for a few minutes until you feel comfortable enough to move. You may use a grounding technique to feel more back in the now. Kneel down and touch the ground. Eat a good soup or root vegetables. You can also hold a grounding crystal during this meditation, like aragonite. Do whatever you feel is most grounding, which for some is listening to music or going for a walk.

I suggest writing this out in steps for yourself and recording it on your phone's voice recorder, then playing it back. If you prefer, have some gentle meditative music playing and diffuse a light essential oil. Don't lie down, as it may cause you to fall asleep, but sit comfortably with pillows supporting you. Green tea can help us to not fall asleep during meditation.

Also, remember that this is best done after you get to the point where you feel compassion for your younger self. If you're not yet feeling compassion, this exercise may not work. Working on self-love in the now is key before travelling in time, but you don't need to be perfect. Becoming a master of self happens over some time and with growth. The inner child work is just another milestone toward stepping into your true power role, but it's a vital step.

You'll find that you'll feel much more comfortable in the following days. If you want to, you can repeat the experience, but I recommend leaving it alone once you've made a good connection. You'll know for sure if it worked for you or not.

If you decide to repeat it, try a different scenario. Try not to revisit the same moment unless you feel you need to say something else. Remember that you're talking to your child self, so use simple language and a calm, respectful tone. Eventually you'll notice that your emotional attachment to your past and your traumas will lessen. Your emotions are calming down a couple of notches, and you'll feel much more in control.

This will also help you to become more observant regarding your thoughts and emotions. Keep a journal and write down your experiences. It will surely make a fantastic book one day, and even if you don't write about it, it's good to do this so you can refer to it years later and remember what you did. We tend to forget things so easily, which is part of the human mind's tragedy.

This is your power. You have the power to heal yourself. When you connect with the parts of you that were stuck in time because of trauma, you allow yourself to merge this part of you for good by acknowledging the pain and sending compassion to yourself. Just like that, you have integrated a part of you to make yourself complete again.

The memory I shared was one of the many fragments I had left behind during my life due to trauma. Recollect your lost fragmented parts to become whole—all of them, connecting through memory and emotions. Be the observer of your past and lend a helping hand to your lost soul part.

This is an important part of the completion and integration process. It wasn't until fall of 2018 that I realized I wasn't the only one who'd experienced this. There were others before me, but it took me until now to understand that it's actually a normal part of the recovery process and a vital part of getting yourself back into one piece.

We can travel through time and space to heal parts of us that we used to believe were currently inaccessible. They aren't inaccessible. That's a lie the matrix wants you to believe to keep you powerless. You're much greater than anyone wants you to believe. The key is to develop and expand your inner space. The ones without inner space aren't capable of doing this. This is, again, why inner-self work is critical.

Heal Yourself

First, you are whole and completely normal. You were traumatized, and because of that you're experiencing life differently than if you'd never been traumatized. Most people experience trauma, and often that's why they can't recognize it as such and will put down those experiences, even telling others to "Suck it up" or "Get over it, drama queen."

You're a whole and healthy human being who experienced something completely abnormal and traumatizing. You responded according to your own human nature, reacting to trauma the only way you can. Essentially, healing yourself is about unlearning the triggers and removing the stress reactions, reducing the effects of the hormones that get triggered, and removing any stress factors that lead you into an alarm response. Healing yourself is about understanding why you react and from where it originates. This means true reasons, not the fake ones people came up with.

You're not the disease with which people labelled you after diagnosing your symptoms. Your symptoms have a cause, and it lies deeply hidden below the surface, under layers and layers of your image of who you are. Healing yourself is about finding your true self and reconnecting with your soul's essence.

The journey of awakening is a personal one, and only you can do this for yourself. You may be looking into modalities and ways to assist yourself during this time, and each of us will intuitively be guided to the right place that will allow us to heal ourselves. Trust God within your own heart to guide you to where you need to be to find and understand yourself.

I began my journey with reiki energy healing many years ago, after my uncle passed away. I felt driven to find a way for us to heal ourselves already back then, as I helplessly stood by while people I loved and cared about perished. I felt that self-healing abilities lie within us and that conventional medicines aren't really helping in the way that they promise.

I took antibiotics between four and six times a year and became more and more resistant to them. It was for bladder infections, which are common in childhood sexual abuse survivors. When I switched over to essential oils for anxiety and began using whole-food supplements, I didn't even have one infection per year.

At the same time, I also began to keep personal boundaries and only made love with my partner when I felt like it. I respected my body when it said no, even if my mind and my partner wanted to. Respecting myself decreased the frequency of my illnesses. Please make sure to respect and love yourself and your body. Don't overextend yourself, and learn to listen to the signs your body sends you. A no is a no.

Reiki and meditation assisted me in my awakening journey. They allowed me to become more open to my spirit and find answers to my questions, which weren't available from other people. There are a lot of misconceptions out there online, and many people talk from a place of ego and righteousness. I want you to learn to find your way back to yourself. Meditate, journal, speak with spirit, talk to the wind, the water, your emotions, and ask spirit within you, then listen to the answers. Those are *your* answers from God, spirit, or your higher self, and they're right for you.

When you begin to help yourself, the angels will cheer you on and also help you on that path. Self-responsibility is extremely empowering, and I want you to learn how to use that tool. It's yours, and God gave it to you. You're supposed to be a self-sovereign being, a divine creation of Mother Earth and our father in heaven, a creation of this universe, so take your power and use it.

This was my angels' message when I was asking why these things happen and where our saviour is, as he'd promised to come back to get us home: "What makes you believe the saviour is not here, walking amongst mankind? He's never left you, but you have. You separated yourselves willingly since the dawn of time. The saviour isn't outside of you. There's one place he resides, and that's within your very own heart. You are your own saviours. You've just forgotten who you are. Wake up and remember."

Beyond Reintegration

You're no longer a survivor but rather someone who thrives. This means you've learned or are learning to cope with the memories of abuse. Over time, you'll find the memories start fading once more, but don't worry, it's okay. You'll learn to live a beautiful life again, or maybe for the first time ever. As you continue to thrive, you can write your story from an observer perspective, no longer reliving anything but being able to write about it and make sense of it all.

Here's your legacy: your immortality and your ability to contribute to the world. We need you, all of us. Each tree is important and vital to our survival and continued thriving. Now is the time to step into your own power role, no matter what you do in your life. You're strong, wise, intelligent, and amazing, so take charge. You're an incredible, loving human being. Become a sovereign being.

Nothing can shake you anymore. Your fears have decreased and disappeared, your hormones are balanced, your mind is clear and focused, and you're able to enjoy life again. Do all the things you've always dreamed of doing. You deserve it, and you were meant to live a beautiful, happy, and joyous life, no matter how old you are now—whether you're 25, 40, 55, or almost 80. Now is your time, not in your past or in your future. Your life is in the now. Enjoy it. Now you can. Finally.

CHAPTER 11

The Key to Changing Our World

O N MANY OCCASIONS, WE ASK ourselves, or God, why things like this happen. What did we do to deserve this? Why do we have to suffer as beings of God's creation? God, why did you abandon us?

The problems we're facing in our world today are not about mental or emotional imbalances. They're also not about climate change or political debates, or about what's moral and what isn't, or what's good or bad, or what's right or wrong. Those are effects we observe related to a bigger underlying problem.

The true cause of all our problems, personal or worldly—as worldly issues directly reflect the problems we struggle with on a more personal level—is unawakened people walking the Earth in denial over their own shadows and the greater truths we're ignoring. This happens when we neglect our being and don't take responsibility for ourselves.

We keep pushing away responsibility onto other people—the government, the neighbour, the abuser, and so on. This isn't at all helpful. Our circumstances may have had an original cause, and we're suffering the effect. Yet healing and growing from that is solely our responsibility and nobody else's.

We can't expect other people to help us or do the work for us. That's not how this works. We have to do that for ourselves, as beings of God. Self-responsibility is what we came here to claim and integrate within our being. All the bullshit that happened shouldn't ever affect the core of our being, the spark of light and love we were born with. Yet it will affect it temporarily, until we remember who we really are at our core and make the decision to claim self-responsibility.

Sometimes we fall into denial of our problems as a way to escape it, without properly addressing it for whatever reason. This leads to us not taking responsibility for our lives. Even abuse has become our responsibility to acknowledge and heal from.

You may say that we need to live, and to live we must move on, and you're right. But what are you building your life upon? You're building it on untruths, denial, and essentially a shaky foundation. Building your city on quicksand leads to destruction at some point, and the dream collapses. Your foundation is key.

I built a good life. I had everything I wanted or thought I wanted, until the day my dream collapsed upon me and I was faced with having to clean up the mess to build anew. This is the universe's proverbial sledgehammer to the head. Eventually, the unreal dissolves to make room for the real. Ask yourself if you're the unreal, or are you simply observing the unreal?

I wasn't going to rebuild my life in the same place or with the same building blocks. I needed to dig deep to find new building blocks that could build a city that could last and be sustainable. That's exactly what we need to do for ourselves as individuals and as humanity at large. We need to rebuild our world with new building blocks that have never yet been used—the new building blocks of greater awareness.

A new way of understanding evolves our being to higher consciousness, resolving personal matters, attitudes, and thoughts triggered by human hormones and programming. By changing perception, we also gain a new way of being and responding. The idea is to not be in resistance to life but to flow with its natural changes, opening our hearts again and connecting to our minds to see with different lenses. This allows for changes from within, the effects seen in our outer world as they reflect our inner world.

So what's the key to resolving world issues? What's the key to having everyone on board to work toward a world that can support growth and peace? The key is inner-self work.

Greta Thunberg told our politicians that they weren't mature enough to lead, and she's correct. You aren't mature enough until you wake up and do your own inner-self work. Only awakened beings are mature enough to lead world governments. Only awakened beings can govern themselves, and that will express into their surroundings. Your awakening is key to changing our world.

We are currently finding ourselves inside the apocalypse that was predicted so many years ago. It's not the end of the world but the end of the old paradigm and the beginning of human awakening. You are laying the groundwork for a new and better future for all living beings on Earth. You're doing this with your own inner-self work and standing in your truth, taking back your power, and leading in new ways never yet explored and experienced.

To return to my dream that was described at the beginning of this book, what do you believe the dream was about, and what do the three pearls represent?

ABOUT ANNCELINE

ANNCELINE ISN'T MY REAL NAME. It's the name I gave my other me—the one who lived through the experiences from my childhood, the part of me I'd repressed. I write under her name about the abuse in order to honour her and respect her as a part of me. It's common for abusers to give the child a different name.

AnnCeline went through a lot, and she protected me from the full realization of my traumas. Without her, I doubt I'd be alive to write this or tell my story. I'm writing it for the many survivors who were labelled bipolar, crazy, schizophrenic, or who knows what. I want to make them realize that their issues have an original cause.

The minute I understood what happened to me, I began to trust myself and stopped feeling like I was losing it. There's usually very little support from family, and people will try to keep us from talking. They will tell us that we wouldn't want our co-workers to know about it, that nobody will believe our story, or that we're being misguided. They might tell us not to talk to our cousins, as their "craziness" could rub off on us—or perhaps that we shouldn't dig into the past, as this isn't good for us. Yet when you remember things and you ask about what happened to you, nobody wants to explain anything. They claim that if you need help, they can help you. Trust me, you don't need that type of help.

I sincerely hope I'm able to break through with my very vulnerable descriptions of the reality I experienced. I had many moments of doubt and wasn't sure if I should publish this at all, because I'm not a psychologist or a medical doctor. I don't have some sort of advanced certificate or a court decision proving that anything I say is accurate. However, I do have my experiences, which are valid and real to me.

I feel that the amount of gaslighting I experienced growing up and also as an adult greatly contributed to my fears of my memories being inaccurate. This is a tactic that many abusers and narcissists will use to confuse you and keep you quiet.

It's important that we drop our fears of being found out. This wasn't our fault, after all. I had to learn to stop covering up for people and stop accepting their bad behaviour. The more we point out the truth and speak up, the more the illusions will dissolve and the lies will no longer have a place to grow and fester in our consciousness.

Our voices and our truths count.

Thank you for reading *A Puzzled Mind*. I hope I was able to shed some light on things and assist you on your own healing journey.

As survivor trees, we reach each other with our branches, creating a protective canopy
for our fellow humans in need of support. We whisper with the wind in the leaves
and connect with our roots underground. You are another me.—AnnCeline

APPENDIX

Methods Used by Child Groomers and Pedophiles

THE FOLLOWING EXAMPLES ARE GATHERED from my personal experiences and memories. This may be very graphic and triggering, so please skip this section if you don't think you'll feel comfortable reading it.

A child being groomed for pedophile abusers and organizations is often being groomed by a close caregiver, like a father or in some cases a mother. It begins with emotional bonding, manipulation, and coercion, then continues with the use of items to enter the vaginal or anal cavities to allow for their widening. This is because they know that the child's condition and the abuse are likely to be discovered by medical professionals if not prepared beforehand to avoid things like tearing of the anal and vaginal cavities and other potential damage. The child may bleed out or even die if this happens. So the children's genitals are slowly being customized to allow the space needed for a penis to fit inside.

At a very young age, a child may be abducted or disappear for a few hours or maybe a day or two, during which time the child will be exposed to rape and sexual abuse by a stranger. This happens early to take away the child's ability to speak due to trauma and shock. The groomer may have already prepared the child beforehand, and at between 4 and 6 years old, the first rape will occur. If it's unsuccessful, they leave it and further prepare the genitals to allow for the rape to happen without tearing or injuring the child.

The combination of emotional bonding and severe abuse creates what we call *trauma bonding*. The abuser will always enter a child's room in the same way. A certain type of knock or a certain word is used that becomes a trigger to put the child into a freeze state. This allows for memories to not be registered properly and explains why you can't pull up the face of the abuser the moment he entered to abuse you, which will make it difficult for you to believe in yourself.

A groomer will pretend to be a great doting father, always changing diapers and babysitting so the mother can have some free time. Please be aware that not all doting fathers are groomers; most are genuinely great and caring fathers. However, you also need to be aware of how groomers work. You may notice a child having a close connection with a groomer suddenly beginning to turn away from the person, becoming scared or easily startled, and preferring to sit with Mom rather than Dad, for example. The child can't explain the reason why, since this is a primal brain response.

Groomers like to use things like candy, money, the promise of a great time, or other rewards to get back the child's trust if they're at risk of losing it. You may notice that sometimes the groomer goes to places with the child. Sometimes he pretends to be visiting friends or eating at a restaurant or going shopping but comes back late, or you may find out later that he didn't go where he said he was going with the child. The child may return asleep or very tired and groggy. The child could also be overly talkative or avoidant.

Child abusers sometimes use drugs to numb the kids and render them unresponsive. The drug that was used during my time was ketamine, the date rape drug. There are signs that can indicate if your child has a ketamine addiction, which may resemble other symptoms as well, so it's not overly recognizable.

Ketamine causes out-of-body experiences, dreamlike memories, hallucinations, feeling jaded, or having an excess amount of shame and guilt that may manifest as anger outbursts or extreme shyness. You may notice a loss of weight, dry skin (especially on the shins), or pale skin and bags under the eyes. As I mentioned earlier, the drug often comes in a white powder form that's put into drinks like cola to hide the taste. Sometimes it comes in tablet or pill form, and children may be told it's their vitamin.

Pedophile organizations often will be like a club. They hide in bars that close for private parties and have tinted windows, so nobody can see inside. Sometimes they pretend to be a ballet school or some other type of organization to make it less obvious. If a group of men arrives with children in ballet outfits, something may not be right, particularly if it's not a well-known and established ballet school. In the nineties. they used to use symbols to mark their establishments online so that other pedophiles would recognize them. Those symbols may now have largely disappeared, as this practice has become known.

Groomers use words and emotions to keep victims under control. He'll try being their friend, giving victims what they want so that they favour him over the other parent. A groomer will try to influence the connection between the child and another caregiver, like the mom, by severing the emotional bond. They'll tell the mom not to hug the child or not check on the child crying in the crib, as that would only allow for emotional bonding between mother and child.

The weaker the bond between mother and child, the more success the abuser has in grooming and sexually abusing the child. Every time the child tries to connect to the mother and explain what happened, the mom's inability to connect emotionally with the child will stop her from taking the child seriously. She may even blame the child for her marital problems. This is caused by the emotional disconnect.

Abusers often target women who are shy or dissociative or known to have been sexual abuse survivors. They often marry women who have a low sex drive and then blame them for issues in the marriage. They use this in cases of confrontation when they get found out. The blame game muffles a partner's ability to speak up and take appropriate action. This delay in taking action toward the pedophile partner eventually leads to severe guilt and shame. It also results in the other partner understanding that if she goes to the police, she may be blamed for not speaking up sooner or even be called an accomplice. This isn't true and in fact was implied by the abuser into the partner victim.

Abusers play an emotional and mental game to get their way. They manipulate children's thoughts and behaviours and make sure they feel emotionally neglected by the other caregiver, to prevent them from disclosing anything. This is called *coercion*, but it may feel to children like they're cursed if they can't remember these details.

In establishments, the pedophiles will teach each other how to groom a child, what to say, and how to behave to make children and other people comply. These are usually very tight-knit organizations, and strangers coming in are thoroughly checked out and investigated. The organizations contain people who can benefit the organization by keeping it secret and safe. If an accident happens, they can take care of it themselves. These include medical doctors, surgeons, lawyers, police officers, judges, and so on—people with money and influence. The Mob may also be involved. I feel that pedophile organizations are criminal gangs that make just as much money as the illegal drug industry. This is a multi-billion-dollar industry that's also tax-free.

Printed in the United States
by Baker & Taylor Publisher Services